The State of Your Church

MEASURING WHAT MATTERS IN MINISTRY

Funding for this research was made possible by the generous support of Gloo. Barna Group was solely responsible for data collection, analysis and writing of the report.

Table of Contents

PREFACE

***Knowing* is foundational to human existence.** To experience the intimacy of being fully known and accepted is essential to every person's growth journey. It's a beautiful thing, and it's biblical. When you look throughout the Bible, you can see the concept woven throughout—being known and allowing oneself to be known. It's how the "big C" church, at a fundamental level, operates: one person seeking to know another and helping them grow, with Christ at the center. A threefold cord.

As ministry leaders, the ability to *know* is paramount to success. Leaders often wonder, "How are my people doing? How effective is my ministry? How am I doing as a leader?" To receive that feedback—the ability to know—is oxygen to any ministry. It helps leaders decide when to stay the course, when to pivot and when to apply interventions.

SCOTT BECK
CEO and founder of Gloo

At Gloo, we've worked with Barna Group in serving thousands of leaders who leverage technology to do just that. We've learned that one of the best ways to gain knowledge is to leverage *common frameworks*—a mutually accepted way of viewing and communicating about something. Common frameworks exist everywhere in the world around us, like the alphabet or metric measurement systems.

Common frameworks help us:
1. See an objective picture of what's happening
2. Measure outcomes and impact, not just activity
3. Allow resources and latent energy to flow

Imagine if doctors measured heart health in 1,000 different ways. It would be very difficult to see how healthy or at-risk a person's heart is. Instead, the medical community agrees on common frameworks like body mass index, cholesterol levels and blood pressure to see an objective picture of health and understand what contributes to and detracts from it. More importantly, those measurements open the aperture into measurable *outcomes* like decreased heart disease and increased longevity.

Here's where it gets interesting: When outcomes can be seen, resources flow.

Imagine a church that starts to measure the emotional health and wellness of its members. The pastor leverages common frameworks to assess how people are doing and gradually makes incremental interventions to improve overall emotional health. Soon, an abundance of latent resources shows up in support of that outcome. Volunteers step up to counsel those in need. Writers, musicians and artists begin to offer their work in support of the emotional flourishing of their church community. More funds, from high-capacity philanthropists to average attendees, are invested as donors see the impact they can make. Every person—in the pews, from behind their screens and in the community at large—can move from consumption to contribution and experience the joy of changing lives.

> "The ability to *know* is oxygen to any ministry. It helps leaders decide when to stay the course, when to pivot and when to apply interventions."

If common frameworks can release the potential energy in a community, then technology can make it scale. Using tools, like digital surveys, content and dashboards, enable knowledge to be transferred and acted on at scale. When used well, technology can decentralize bottlenecks and create efficiencies. Surveys make it easy for would-be leaders to raise their hand, and help beyond-busy pastors build capacity. Dashboards and reports can inspire potential donors and volunteers to meet needs with their time and treasure.

As we acknowledge the digitally native environment in which we live, we can't ignore technology. On the contrary, I believe it's a moral imperative for us to selectively use the tools we have at hand, ultimately for his purposes.

Here, in *The State of Your Church*, you'll be learning about common frameworks like human flourishing and church thriving. You'll also be introduced to assessment technologies, powered by Gloo, to put these concepts to work and see the state of your church, city, or community. These tools, like the ChurchPulse, are designed to be a tactic in *your* strategy and release the latent energy that sits right within your pews.

Bringing this work into realization is no small task, and I'm grateful for Barna CEO David Kinnaman's willingness to give his time, talents and resources to it, all while going through very challenging times in his own life. David's heart for the Church is unwavering, and he excels at stewarding the role Barna is uniquely qualified to fill. The entire Barna team, every single person, has contributed their personal passion and talents to bring this work to fruition. And the Gloo team has stepped in with creativity and servant leadership to wholeheartedly support Barna in this effort.

As you embark upon this journey, my prayer for you is that you would be abundantly blessed with insight and the inspiration to put these tools to work in your church as you experience the joy of a flourishing and thriving community. ●

HOW TO USE **THIS BOOK**

The State of Your Church equips pastors and church leaders with simple insights and tools to become experts of their own church environment.

In some ways, this book is the culmination of decades of Barna research, illuminating new frameworks for measuring what matters in ministry. Barna CEO David Kinnaman sets the stage with a vision for a renewed Church and advice for using data well in your context (page 10).

Importantly, Barna senior fellow Rev. Dr. Glenn Packiam then reflects on what it means to be a resilient pastor (page 20). Recent data show that pastors are more at risk than ever for burnout. We don't want this book to feel like "just one more thing" you should read and apply; we want to help you, and those you lead, remain strong and healthy in the face of ongoing, unprecedented challenges.

With that foundation laid, we'll spend the following sections unpacking key categories for measuring ministry. You might want to gradually make your way through these sections or consult them to better understand specific needs in your congregation.

The section on **Flourishing People** focuses on individuals and their personal growth in five domains of life: faith, relationships, vocation, finances and well-being. We'll probe deeper into the connection between being part of a church community and human flourishing.

The section on **Thriving Churches** focuses on your church as a whole, with 15 proposed measurements for congregational health. You'll find a number of pathways to see how your ministry is nurturing, sending and leading people toward a robust life of faith.

Along the way, we'll share contributions from practitioners, including **Q&As** with real-world advice from experts and **field guides** learning from other churches that are embracing data-informed strategy and ministry.

If you want to sit with the numbers, there is an extensive series of **data tables** (beginning page 108) looking at the research on flourishing and thriving among some select demographic groups. The data Barna has gleaned from surveys represent churches of all regions, denominations and sizes, ensuring that you're benchmarking your church against a truly representative data set. If you're curious to learn more about how we conduct these studies and what certain terms in our data storytelling mean, just flip to the **Methodology** and **Glossary** (page 148). ●

Throughout the book, you'll see QR codes that will take you to additional resources and interviews curated by the Barna team. Just hold your phone's camera or QR code reader over the square to open the related link.

The State of Your Church *should be helpful as a stand-alone resource, but it's especially designed to go along-side Barna's free ChurchPulse assessment. To use the assessment, or to make the most of some of the other bonus content, you will need a free account on Barna Access, our subscription service.*

A VISION FOR
A RENEWED CHURCH

DAVID KINNAMAN
CEO of Barna Group

It's a new day for ministry.

Don't you think it's time to shake off the haze and brush away the cobwebs?

After all church leaders have endured in the last few years, many of us are ready for new ideas and fresh paradigms. Barna consistently hears from leaders who are more eager than ever to try new approaches to forming souls in the way of Jesus. The pandemic and other disruptions have reminded us that many of the people we thought of as loyal churchgoers were just not that into the church. Although ministry was never exactly easy in the past, we more fully understand the challenges to effective discipleship. The approaches we thought were foolproof just aren't working in the way they used to.

I firmly believe this moment provides an opportunity to pioneer new ways of leading God's people and new, deeper pathways to discipling people.

It's a *kairos* moment. An opportunity to fashion new wineskins, as Jesus suggested we do.[1] A chance to seek the Lord's heart for more of what he desires. Of course, God is still changing lives. And he seeks to do that through the Church, through *your church*.

So, this key moment for the Church raises key questions:

- What is the state of *your church?*
- How thriving is it? Think of "thriving" as the organizational dynamics of the church. How well is that going?
- How are people doing in your church? Are they flourishing or not?
- How are *you* doing? What's the state of your heart?
- And, perhaps as crucial, *how* do you know? What means do you employ to measure what matters in ministry?

God is always doing new things in the world (see Isaiah 43:19). What a privilege it is for us to leverage this moment to pursue a renewed and revived Christian community.

Measuring What Matters

This book describes both a mindset and a method to address these questions, to hopefully bring you closer than ever to why you got into ministry in the first place. To transform lives! To build a thriving church! All while starting strong and finishing well as a leader.

The State of Your Church is a guidebook to help you and your team take stock of (1) how much your church is thriving, (2) the degree to which the people in your church are flourishing and (3) how you're doing as a leader.

The State of Your Church stems from a decades-long journey here at Barna. In the last few years especially, we've been diligently working on frameworks for measuring what matters, with the incredible team at Gloo, led by Scott Beck.

We've approached this whole effort in a way that honors the unique distinctives across the broader Church (e.g., denominationally, theologically); we've done our best not to force-fit anything. We want you to bring your own ministry DNA to this book and the associated tools. That's the whole point: We are not focusing solely on the state of *the* Church but also equipping you with tools for understanding the state of *your* church.

> "We want you to bring your own ministry DNA to this book and the associated tools"

Before you can create a new model for measuring what matters, you have to first decide what matters. Borrowing from Frederick Buechner's Venn diagram for determining personal calling and vocation, today's churches need to merge their great, driving passion (the Great Commission) with the world's great need (finding deep satisfaction and rest for our souls).[2] In this intersection, you'll be able to see more clearly what your calling is as a church. When you're clear on your calling as a church, you can start to define and refine the data you'll look for as indicators that people's lives are being transformed.

> "Transformation isn't a linear progression, and measuring people's inner change doesn't always lead up and to the right"

The challenge, of course, is that the work of the Holy Spirit isn't necessarily quantifiable. Sometimes spiritual growth looks a lot like going backward. When we grow in Christ, measuring outcomes might actually look like people are more humble, more willing to admit their challenges, more willing to talk about their shortcomings. Transformation isn't a linear progression, and measuring people's inner change doesn't always lead up and to the right.

Shifting Toward a Renewed Church

What is required of leaders and pastors to renew the Church in these confusing and complex times?

Here are five shifts I believe we need to consider:

1. **A renewed Church requires Christian leaders who honestly and objectively evaluate the impact they are making.** The most effective leaders are consistently seeking input and evaluation of their ministry models in order to be more faithful. It's essentially a matter of stewardship. And the stakes are extremely high: Jesus warns that it would be better for us to be weighted to the bottom of the sea than for us to mislead those to whom we minister. What a responsibility to get this right! Ministry impact and ministry models should be subjected to the same kind of rigor. For example, as Barna has found that two in three young people raised as Christians will walk away from the Church as they enter young adulthood, leaders should spend more time wondering how to fix this massive dropout problem and less time explaining it away as "just a fact of life" or "the way

it's always been." A renewed Church is going to demand more thoughtful, intentional effort to make the kind of difference we really intend to make, through the power of the gospel.

2. **A renewed Church needs leaders who are in tune with the flourishing of the people they are serving and discipling.** Even with the luxury of full sanctuaries and active attendance patterns, we can't be sure how people are faring and how much they are growing in the Lord. While there are always limitations to research, I believe that we have a responsibility to better understand the flourishing of people. First, Jesus' words and the broader sweep of the New Testament place a high calling on the role of shepherding and, I contend, knowing people is an essential part of shepherding them. Second, the tools exist to enable you to do just this—even to do so in a way that honors people's privacy—and they are powerful and easy to use. Of course, just because you *can* do something doesn't mean that you should. But if assessment capabilities and insights allow you to be more faithful in your ministry, it's worth considering. Since it is so easy to rely on assumptions or muscle memory or a few anecdotes, I am convinced that effective leadership will require even better ways of hearing from people. Leaders need a new way to measure a church's influence on people's *whole* lives, not just the Sunday morning context. Innovations in technology have allowed us to gather data and glean insights in ways never before possible. This book will introduce you to just some of the innovations Barna has been able to take part in, with the help of our partners at Gloo, and how they can serve you as you serve your church.

3. **A renewed Church requires contributors and participants in gospel mission, not just consumers of gospel content.** I believe this is one of the key shifts we need to prioritize coming out of the last few years: The Church must become better at developing people and releasing them in their giftedness. Some of our recent studies show that 92 percent of pas-

tors prefer lay-driven initiatives to new church programs and 96 percent say that for their church to be healthier, lay people must take more responsibility. Yet only 9 percent of pastors say their church is very effective at developing new leaders and only a small minority of churchgoers says their church has helped them to identify and use their giftedness. What's wrong with this picture? While pastors are to be commended for all they've held together the last few years, we can no longer rely so heavily or solely on professional ministers. Another way to say this is that effective ministry will require a shift to significantly upgrade the equipping and releasing of the priesthood of *all* believers.

4. **A renewed Church needs leaders who are self-aware about the condition of their hearts before the Lord**. A consistent theme of the scriptures is what my friend Ed calls "heart health." I find the numerous biblical references to God's care for our hearts to be one of the most compelling parts of Christian witness. This ancient book seems to be written way ahead of its time. It speaks to a God who cares about the deepest crevices and cracks in the walls of humanity. It describes a God who cares much more about the human heart than about mere behavior. Leaders have perhaps an even greater responsibility than do others to tend to their hearts, because their leadership has the power to enhance or cloud people's ability to see the light of Jesus.

5. **A renewed Church demands that we rely more on the Lord's power and presence than on our strategy or smarts.** This is a book about the ins and outs of research and assessment; as such, it's a book for geeks and for those who want to know what's working and why. Yet it's also a book about letting our strategic efforts provide a vessel through which the Holy Spirit can work. Paul writes that he came not with wise and persuasive words, but with a demonstration of the Spirit's power. I am convinced that, more than ever, a revived Church is going to require a commitment to making way for people to experience God's

power and presence. This may require us to unlearn and relearn some things as we, like John the Baptist, become lesser so that Jesus can become greater.

Developing a Theology of Success

In addition to these five shifts, let's explore some of the key commitments we can make on the road to exploring the state of *your* church. If the five shifts describe something of the destination—a vision of a desireable future for the Church—we might think of these as some of the stars by which we navigate.

When we talk about measuring what matters, we must keep these principles in mind.

1. Success in God's economy is faithfulness.
2. Some things, especially in the realm of spirituality, are very hard to measure.
3. Many things can—and should—be measured.
4. Big can be great, but bigger is not always better.
5. When things look bleak, God can still be working.
6. We need to be willing to stop what we're doing and go in a different direction.
7. Even as we develop a theology of success, we need a theology of failure.

The latter reminds me of a story about my father, Gary Kinnaman. He led a church in the Phoenix area for nearly three decades. The church experienced steady growth for nearly all those years, becoming one of the largest churches in metro Phoenix. Yet, in the final years before he left, the church began to experience declines in giving and attendance. One day, over lunch with a close friend and confidant, he drew a back-of-the-napkin graph of the growth and decline.

"I don't know what else to try. After decades of knowing what to do to help grow this church, I feel like my options and ideas are running thin. I just can't figure out how to reverse the declines of the last few years," lamented my father to his friend.

"Well, Gary, look at the drops in attenders and dollars," he said as he pointed across the table at my dad's drawing. "That's not your fault. So don't take these downward shifts so personally."

He paused for that to sink in, then added, "And these many years of incredible growth? Those aren't your doing. Your ideas and energy may have been part of what God used to build this church. You don't get credit for them. God does."

I've heard my father tell that story many times, because it was such an important reset for him as he sought to lead faithfully. And it's a reminder of the first principle of measuring what matters. God cares first and foremost about faithfulness.

It's a reminder of Paul's admonition in 1 Corinthians 15:58 (NLT): "Always work enthusiastically for the Lord, for you know that nothing you do for the Lord is ever useless."

Remembering Our Roots

Renewing the Church will mean getting back to basics, including our first sense of calling to ministry. Pastors don't typically devote their lives to ministry out of a vision to merely monitor attendance and weekly giving. No, they're drawn to serve the Church to fulfill Jesus' mandate to "go and make disciples of all nations, baptizing them in the name of the Father and of the Son and of the Holy Spirit, and teaching them to obey everything I have commanded you" (Matthew 28: 19–20).

Pastors and church leaders all get into ministry to make a difference.

To change lives.

To see people transformed into the way of Jesus.

However, somewhere along the line, the vision to help people discover and know Jesus and experience the power of the Holy Spirit working in their lives gets blurred. We mistake operational, attendance and engagement metrics as our chief measurements of success in the church.

Instead of tracking progress toward the Great Commission—measuring spiritual growth, love in action and new growth emerging from baptized disciples—we monitor building costs, staff budgets and operational expenses against weekly attendance and giving. Those are important metrics, but they are not the main thing.

For too long, this scoreboard has driven the Church's playbook. But the game has changed dramatically, especially in the past two decades. Data tell a new story about how people are growing in their faith. "Executive" data, like attendance and revenue, don't fully capture the shifting sands of culture.

Added to ongoing and significant societal changes in practices and beliefs about churchgoing (which have led to a continual decline in attendance), the pandemic has also altered the way people engage with their local church. It forced church leaders to do some deep soul-searching on the role of the local church in people's lives: *Why does it matter if people come to church? What is the primary purpose of church? How can today's generations flourish in their faith when they are increasingly disengaged and disinterested in church? How can you measure people's spiritual growth to know if what you're doing at church is making an impact on their lives?*

> "We mistake operational, attendance and engagement metrics as our chief measurements of success in the church"

While the pandemic created its own new set of challenges for church leaders (becoming an online church was brand new and no small feat for most churches in America!), it also revealed one major, uncomfortable truth about our present culture's view of the Church: People "just aren't that into you," to borrow a phrase from the world of dating. A lot of people have indicated, both by their absence and their lack of engagement in online or in-person church programs that being part of and growing in a community of faith simply isn't their top priority in life. For some, being a disciple at all has diminished in importance. And yet churches spend so much time, effort and money creating programs to draw people in. To help them find and form a deep faith.

What's a pastor to do in this climate of confusing cultural change and disruption in the Church? First and foremost, leaders need to reclaim their mission and vision for *why* church matters—what the Church's role is for bringing lasting bread and living water to a starved, parched world—and then build a system to measure whether they're making disciples and baptizing them, literally and figuratively, into new life.

The Biblical Case for Seeking Input

Another part of seeking a renewed Church is understanding that, now more than ever, we can't just operate on ministry autopilot. We need input in the form of research, data, insight, advice, counsel, discernment and wisdom.

Scripture gives us plenty of examples of how ministry leaders used research and data to help inform major decisions. Take Moses, for example. In Numbers 13, he commissions a research project to explore Canaan: "'See what the land is like and whether the people who live there are strong or weak, few or many. What kind of land do they live in? Is it good or bad? What kind of towns do they live in? Are they unwalled or fortified? How is the soil? Is it fertile or poor? Are there trees in it or not? Do your best to bring back some of the fruit of the land'" (Numbers 13: 18–20).

After running a 40-day field survey, they returned to Moses, Aaron and the whole assembly and reported their findings: "We went into the land to which you sent us, and it does flow with milk and honey! Here is its fruit. But the people who live there are powerful, and the cities are fortified and very large. We even saw descendants of Anak there. The Amalekites live in the Negev; the Hittites, Jebusites and Amorites live in the hill country; and the Canaanites live near the sea and along the Jordan" (Numbers 13: 27–29).

Armed with this data, Caleb suggests they occupy Canaan. The field researchers don't like this idea and try to talk their leaders out of it. In the end, Moses and Aaron obey God and forge ahead to Canaan, albeit with great angst and opposition within their ranks.

> Ministry leaders can't afford *not* to use credible information and evidence to help inform the direction they want to take as a ministry and to help monitor the effects of their decisions

As a social researcher, this chapter warms my heart. Moses understood the power of godly, realistic input for decision-making, especially when the stakes are high and you're leading people into new territory. The Old Testament includes many other examples of leaders and people of God sending teams out to gather and use intelligence, often to "spy out the land" before entering (see Joshua 2:24, Judges 7:10–18 and Nehemiah 2:11–16, for instance).

Scripture is full of its own data that show God wants us to think well about how we conduct our lives and how we help others find faith and grow in it. Ministry leaders can't afford *not* to use credible information and evidence to help inform the direction they want to take as a ministry and to help monitor the effects of their decisions.

At Barna, we often refer to Issachar, a tribe that, 1 Chronicles 12:32 tells us "understood the times" and knew what to do. Social research as we know it today is more sophisticated, but its purpose is often the same: to understand the times and know what to do. This isn't just a biblical precedent, but a pressing need for the Church at large—and for your church too—in an era in which people are drifting away from and questioning the relevance of faith.

> "Healthy leaders, flourishing individuals, a thriving Body of Christ—it's a beautiful picture of the Church, isn't it?"

Data should matter to faith leaders because people matter. Through this lens, percentages become glimpses into the backgrounds, beliefs, challenges and hopes of individuals. They become tools to better understand the world around us and how your people, your church and you as their leader exist within it.

Based on the data we've been compiling for this project since 2019, we've observed a virtuous cycle: Flourishing people help build a thriving congregation, which is sustained by a healthy leader, who invests in the flourishing of individuals ... and on it goes. Healthy leaders, flourishing individuals, a thriving Body of Christ—it's a beautiful picture of the Church, isn't it? Doesn't it feel closer to what Jesus was inviting us to build when he handed over the keys to the Kingdom?

We want to help you better understand and measure what matters for the sake of gospel transformation. The disruptions in today's world and in the Church go deeper than we imagine, but that also means the opportunities for ministry are richer and more unexpected than many perceive. We firmly believe in the work of the local church, and we want to see people and pastors flourish and their churches thrive.

The challenges of leading the people of God are formidable, and still the opportunities for community transformation, personal flourishing and a renewed Church are surprisingly bright. With creative problem-solving and innovative thinking, together we can "spy out the land" and take new ground. ●

START BY **CULTIVATING RESILIENT LEADERS**

REV. DR. GLENN PACKIAM
Pastor, author, Barna senior fellow

The late rabbi Lord Jonathan Sacks described going for a medical exam upon being named Chief Rabbi in the British Commonwealth.[3] Part of the exam involved time on a treadmill. As the doctor kept increasing the pace, Sacks was curious what the goal was. "What are you testing?" he asked. "How fast I can go or how long?" Bracing himself to either pick up speed or settle in for a long jog, Sacks was surprised by his doctor's response. "Neither."

Instead, the doctor informed him, he was being evaluated to see how quickly his pulse would return to normal after coming off the treadmill. This is one of the key markers of health: the rate of recovery. The goal of a stress test is to see how someone deals with it.

So it is in life. We cannot eliminate all occasions for angst or anxiety, but we can find out how we hold up during the storm. We can take note of the toll stress exacts from us.

One might call this resilience—the ability to bounce back, to get back up, to persevere, to keep going. But resilience is difficult, and for leaders it can feel impossible. After all, leadership is, on some level, the willingness to live in a state of stress—the stress of bearing the weight of other people's hopes and dreams, of bearing the brunt of the projections of other leaders' failures and shortfalls, of shouldering the burden of responsibility and of decision-making. For the 38 percent of pastors who told Barna in late 2021 that they had seriously considered quitting full-time ministry, that might feel like cold comfort.[4]

A Word to the Weary

Sometimes, leadership can feel like more than a human can possibly bear. As Rabbi Sacks reminded us, four men we might con-

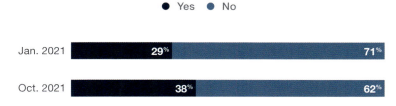

America's Pastors on Their Future in Full-Time Ministry

Have you given real, serious consideration to quitting being in full-time ministry within the last year?

● Yes ● No

Jan. 2021	29%	71%
Oct. 2021	38%	62%

n=413 U.S. Protestant pastors, January 22–27, 2021;
n=507 U.S. Protestant pastors, October 12–28, 2021.

sider spiritual giants in the Hebrew scriptures—Moses, Elijah, Jeremiah and Jonah—all prayed that God would take their life rather than ask them to continue in their task.

Before talking about what it looks like to cultivate resilience, I want to speak to those who are seriously struggling with their mental and emotional health. In fact, I want to say three things specifically and clearly: It's OK to not be OK. It's OK to ask for help. And it's OK to step away from ministry in order to heal. When you can't just bounce back or carry on, when you feel like you can't persevere, this is not automatically a flaw or failure of Christian character. Many times, it just means the wound is deeper than you had realized. Sometimes pain is inflicted upon us; other times pain is a sickness deep inside us. Often, it's a mix of both. Either way, we are not well. The inability to recover—the lack of resilience—is not the problem; it's a symptom.

If that's you, please find a counselor. If you're married, take time away together, either on your own or at a guided retreat or marriage intensive. Ask—tenderly but boldly—for a sabbatical, even if it's for a few months. It is not your Christian duty to soldier on; it is your Christ-like calling to be whole.

There is life beyond "the ministry." There is a world beyond the local church. And there is a "you" beyond your vocation. A counselor might describe this recognition as healthy *differentiation*, knowing the difference between you and the ministry you do or the church you lead. Normally, differentiation is applied to a relationship between two people. If on the one side is *enmeshment*, where one swallows up the other, or the two have gotten inextricably tangled and lost in each other, on the other side is a kind of *detachment*, where a person refuses to be affected or moved by another. Differentiation is the word for being able to be close to another person while remaining yourself.

It applies to pastors and our churches too. We can become enmeshed with our churches. You see this when pastors refer to the congregation as "my people" or "my sheep" or when, referring to things the church or a team has accomplished, they say "I did that." It is also why some pastors threaten whistle-blowers or truth-tellers with a warning that if leadership is brought down, the church will fall with them. They can't envision the church without them, and they can't envision themselves without the church.

> ## "It is not your Christian duty to soldier on; it is your Christ-like calling to be whole"

Pastors can also become detached from their churches, though I suspect this is not as likely. We stop caring about the particular people or their particular situations and just deliver generic words and offer vague platitudes. Our lips are moving, but our hearts are far away. Barna's research reveals that some of the pastors who are most burned out have been in ministry for about 20 years but at their particular church for only about seven years. I wonder, is it possible they have been in ministry long enough to be weary, but have been at one local church too briefly to be rooted in love? I'm not sure. But I suspect the temptation to detach from the church grows when we move, for whatever reason, from one church to the next.

A healthy differentiation allows us to love our churches, to care for our people, to find joy in exercising our gifts for the glory of God and the good of others and to know that the ministry is not our identity. We are not the churches we lead or the sermons we preach. We are beloved children of God.

The Majority of Pastors Recalls Being Called

Can you recall a definitive moment in your life when you were "called" into the ministry?

● Yes   ● No

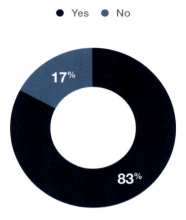

17%

83%

n=408 U.S. Protestant pastors, September 16–October 8, 2020.

Resilience Begins with a Renewed Love

Resilience is not something we conjure up. As Christians, we should reject any notion that resilience means pulling ourselves up by our own bootstraps or finding a way to tough it out. Resilience, when it shows up in our lives, is a work of grace. In fact, the Christian word for what we're trying to name with a word like resilience is *faithfulness*—steadfast, enduring, persevering love.

Paul calls faithfulness a fruit of the Spirit. But like every work of the Spirit, our participation is invited. There is a mystery to this, but we must be clear that God is the author, the sustainer and the finisher of the work. Somewhere along the way, we, by the grace of God and by the Spirit's power, get to join in. We are drawn into the trinitarian life of God, immersed in his love, and participate in who he is and what he is doing. So, when I speak of cultivating resilience, it's important that we know that this is what *God* is cultivating in us. Paying attention to God and cooperating with him in his work is the mystery of both spiritual formation and Christian mission.

Resilience, then, begins with Jesus. It certainly did for Peter. Peter started strong; he had received revelation from the Father that Jesus was the Messiah. He was bold in his promise to never turn away from Jesus, even though he didn't understand that Jesus was heading for the cross. In the moment of testing, in a time of turbulence, when Peter's world was being turned upside down—as the Messiah was arrested by the Romans—Peter failed. He denied Jesus three times. After the resurrection, Jesus appeared to his disciples— but even so, Peter seemed shaken. He returned to fishing, not automatically a sign that he had given up on his vocation as a leader in this new assembly of Jesus followers, but surely a sign that he had lost his nerve.

> "We are not the churches we lead or the sermons we preach. We are beloved children of God."

When Jesus came to Peter, there on the shores of the Sea of Galilee, he seemed to be closely reenacting the scene of Peter's first call, when a failure to catch fish was met by a miraculous turn of events at Jesus' word.

Then comes the question: "Peter, do you love me?"

Surely Peter understood that Jesus was renewing Peter's call. Yet this time the call was not, "Follow me and I will make you a fisher of men." This time there was no word about purpose or cause or mission. It was a word of love. While preachers strain out meaning from the different Greek words for *love*, the only word used in both instances of Peter's calling is the word *me*. Not, "Do you love the church or the sheep?" Or, "Do you love my teaching?" Or even, "Do you love the Kingdom?" or "Do you love the miracles and the movement of God?" It was simply and clearly about Jesus.

Do you love me?

The love of a church or a calling can't keep us from falling. Our first love is not a purpose, but a person: Jesus himself. Resilience begins with a renewed love for Jesus.

Resilience Is Reinforced by the Right Relationships

I have made the mistake of thinking that I couldn't be proactive about friendships. This wasn't a conscious thought, of course. But the realization came to me as I sat in a conference led by Pete and Geri Scazzero in Queens. We had been given an assignment to fill out a "rule of life," a modern iteration of an ancient practice of outlining rhythms and practices for different areas of life. I had no trouble writing down the habit of my work or prayer or even of rest. But the final category had me stumped. I had no intentional rhythms of relationship. And that's when it hit me: I had subconsciously believed that I couldn't, not because I didn't deserve to but because I couldn't afford to. I had to give my time to those who asked.

Pastoral ministry is relational work that often involves an illusion of intimacy. I say "illusion" because we are there with people in their most vulnerable and intimate moments—preparing for marriage, welcoming a child, dealing with the shame of failure or the fracturing of a relationship. We see people through their eruptions of joy or fountains of tears, at life's brightest moments and its darkest hours. But we are not often there for the humdrum of daily life. We're not typically the football-game-watching buddy or Sunday-lunch friend for most people.

This inconsistent intimacy takes a toll. It requires what sociologist Arlie Hochschild referred to as "surface acting"—where we change the emotion that we display—or, more often, "deep acting"—where we summon up the actual feelings from within.[5] Work in service industries, like being a flight attendant (whom Hochschild studied) or waiting tables or dealing with customers, requires surface acting. But empathy work, like counseling or ministry, requires deep acting. We *must* meet people where they are emotionally. By the time we're done for the day, we may not have much left for other relationships.

A second challenge for pastors is the time it takes to cultivate relationships. Friendships are usually formed in leisure hours. In two groundbreaking studies from the University of Kansas published in the *Journal of Social and Personal Relationships* in 2018, communication studies professor Jeffrey Hall found that it takes "between 40 and 60 hours to form a casual friendship, 80–100 hours to transition to being a friend and more than 200 hours together to become good friends."[6] According to Hall's study, the hours spent at work together don't count as much. There's no getting around it, however. We need meaningful friendships if we're going to last in ministry and if we're going to stay fully human, and cultivating those friendships takes time.

It's also important to think about making the *right* relationships.

As the apostle Paul discovered, people will let us down. There is no one best friend, one co-laborer in the Lord who will never leave. After John Mark deserted Paul and Barnabas, we might think that Paul found Silas and never looked back. But the picture is more complex than that. As Paul's letters themselves show, there was a constellation of voices who guided and supported Paul, strengthening him at various points of his life and ministry. We imagine Paul as a heroic individual, striking out on his own through stormy seas and desert roads, planting churches, preaching publicly and enduring persecution. But Paul was never truly on his own. At Paul's lowest moments, God met him not only in prayer and worship but through people as well.

In one of Paul's most vulnerable letters, Paul describes how God's comfort came when he was shaken and discouraged: "God comforts people who are discouraged, and he comforted us by Titus' arrival. We weren't comforted only by his arrival but also by the comfort he had received from you" (2 Corinthians 7:6–7). It was a chain of love, the dynamic force of fellowship. Paul lasted because of the grace of God and the people God placed around him.

We need sages to advise us, leaders to direct us or hold us accountable, peers to remind us that we aren't alone, healers to dress our wounds and companions who carry us when we can't carry on.

Resilience is reinforced by the right relationships. And cultivating these relationships means moving beyond the illusion of intimacy and taking the time to seek out a constellation of lives that help us navigate the stormy seas of life and ministry.

Resilience Is Rooted in the Hope of Resurrection

Above all, the reason resilience is possible is that Jesus Christ is risen from the dead. When Paul was writing to the Church in Corinth, rife with their own issues and struggles, he concludes his letter by reminding them of the resurrection. If Jesus Christ is not risen from the dead, he says, then their preaching and their faith has been in vain.

The only thing that would make our ministry a waste is if Jesus is still in the grave. And if Jesus is dead, then it wouldn't just be the work of pastors but the faith of every Christian that would be for naught. If the benefit of Christianity were just existential—a positive effect on our outlook and behavior—then "we are of all people most to be pitied" (1 Corinthians 15:19, NRSV).

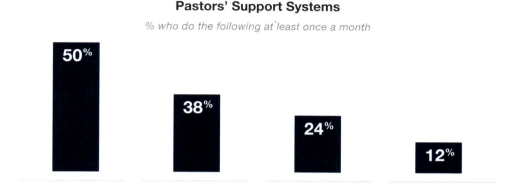

Pastors' Support Systems

% who do the following at least once a month

50%	38%	24%	12%
Receive some form of direct spiritual support	Talk with someone about your emotional and mental health	Meet with a spiritual director / mentor	Meet with a counselor

n=408 U.S. Protestant pastors, September 16–October 8, 2020.

But Jesus isn't still in the grave. Jesus Christ is risen from the dead! Therefore, our faith is not vain, and neither is our preaching. Victory—over sin, death and guilt—is coming in totality, and "all will be made alive in Christ" (1 Corinthians 15:22b, NRSV). Those who are in Christ will receive resurrection bodies.

> "Seek out a constellation of lives to help you navigate the stormy seas of life and ministry"

Paul's pastoral exhortation flows from this hope. We are to live sober and sensible lives, knowing that what we do matters and that bad company corrupts good character (1 Corinthians 15:33). We cannot simply eat and drink and be merry. We must live circumspectly. Then, at the end of the chapter, Paul speaks not just to our lives but to our labor. "Therefore, my beloved, be steadfast, immovable, always excelling in the work of the Lord, because you

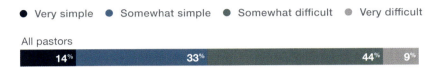

Pastors' Spiritual Investment in Themselves

How simple or difficult is it for you to find time in your ministry schedule to invest in your own spiritual development?

● Very simple   ● Somewhat simple   ● Somewhat difficult   ● Very difficult

All pastors

| 14% | 33% | 44% | 9% |

n=408 U.S. Protestant pastors, September 16–October 8, 2020.

know that in the Lord your labor is not in vain" (1 Corinthians 15:58, NRSV). Because Jesus Christ is risen from the dead, our labor is not vain.

How are these things connected? What is it about the resurrection that grounds our resilience? I think there are at least two things to be said. The first is that resurrection reminds us that, as Frederick Buechner put it, the worst thing is never the last thing.[7] No matter what happens, it will not be the end. The church may fail, your job may end, you might move on to live out your calling in a new or unconventional way. But because we serve the God who raises the dead, nothing we have done in the Lord will be wasted.

There's something else. Resurrection also puts things in perspective. We are playing the long game here. Paul was writing to a particular local church almost 2,000 years ago. And here we still are, gathering on the Lord's day all around the world, calling people to worship, proclaiming the good news and inviting others to follow Jesus. The Church was here long before us, and the Church will be here long after us. As my senior pastor and friend, Brady Boyd, is fond of saying, we are all interim pastors.

This is a point that was driven home powerfully when I saw a picture of the plaque on the wall of a friend's church in England. It lists the names of all the vicars who have served that congregation. The list begins in 1326, with Robert de Marton, and goes all the way to 2010. My friend, Dominic, is the vicar now. The testament of this plaque reminded me that we don't have to change the world or be dramatic or epic or spectacular. We simply need to be faithful—to be "steadfast, immovable, always excelling in the work of the Lord."

A Prayer for Pastors

Resilience is a sign of health, but it is also a work of grace. It is only possible because we are deeply and truly loved, because we have been drawn into the life of the triune God. There we can be healed; there our first love can be renewed; there we can share in life-giving relationships with others where we give and receive love.

So, my prayer for you, dear pastor, is what Paul prayed for the Ephesians:

I pray that, according to the riches of his glory, he may grant that you may be strengthened in your inner being with power through his Spirit, and that Christ may dwell in your hearts through faith, as you are being rooted and grounded in love. I pray that you may have the power to comprehend, with all the saints, what is the breadth and length and height and depth, and to know the love of Christ that surpasses knowledge, so that you may be filled with all the fullness of God.

Now to him who by the power at work within us is able to accomplish abundantly far more than all we can ask or imagine, to him be glory in the church and in Christ Jesus to all generations, forever and ever. Amen. (Ephesians 3:16-21, NRSV) ●

Watch Glenn Packiam share more about the importance of self-care in leadership.

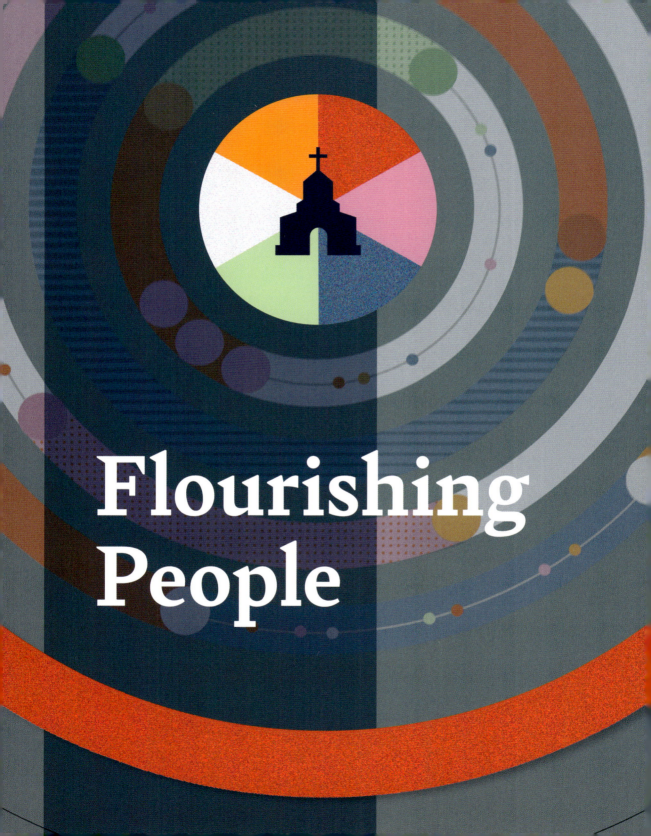

Flourishing People

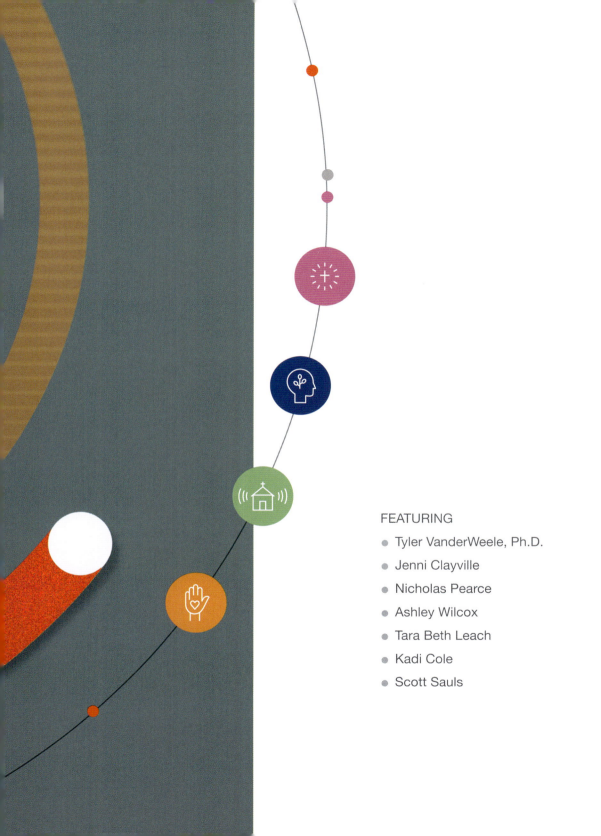

FEATURING

- Tyler VanderWeele, Ph.D.
- Jenni Clayville
- Nicholas Pearce
- Ashley Wilcox
- Tara Beth Leach
- Kadi Cole
- Scott Sauls

WHY FLOURISHING PEOPLE MATTER

As we look toward the renewal of the Church and pursue it in our own communities, research encourages us to pay closer attention to how people are *really* doing and in what ways they are growing, stuck or deficient.

Barna's work on this topic is just one contribution to a broad and growing field of study. Scientists and researchers such as Harvard University's Tyler J. VanderWeele have examined the topic of human flourishing in depth. Typically, these studies approach flourishing through the lens of relationships, vocation, finances and physical and mental well-being.[8] Fascinatingly, research such as VanderWeele's repeatedly shows that individuals whose lives are grounded in faith and who maintain connection to an active church community are more likely to flourish in the other key dimensions of life. (Learn more on page 57 in a Q&A with VanderWeele.)

In a 2021 piece for *Christianity Today* titled "Empty Pews Are a Public Health Crisis," VanderWeele and Brendan Case write, "People find their social and personal lives improved—sometimes their lives are even physically saved—when they go to church often."[9]

It calls to mind scriptures like Psalm 92:12 ("The righteous will flourish like a palm tree"), alluding to the strength found in a life of faithfulness.

Barna recommends that church leaders understand their own capacity to promote holistic health in their congregations and become more aware of how spiritual formation and church attendance have meaningful connections to the flourishing of individuals.

For nearly four decades, Barna has developed a deep well of data to draw from in understanding the impact of a vital faith on people's lives. We'll point to those trends and research foundations in this book. More recently, since 2019, we have been hard at work alongside analysts at Gloo to create a framework for Christian leaders to make the necessary connections between faith and human flourishing.

This book shows the results of that extensive exploration, especially among churchgoers. You'll find national norms and patterns across five areas or "dimensions" of human flourishing— **faith, relationships, vocation, finances and well-being**—as well as powerful insights into how you can measure the degree of flourishing among individuals in your church.

The framework for these five flourishing dimensions is available through our Barna ChurchPulse tool, an assessment which allows you to check in with your congregants holistically and anonymously.

Become more aware of how spiritual formation and church attendance have meaningful connections to the flourishing of individuals

There are a few ways we'll discuss the results of our nationally representative research on human flourishing. Each of the five dimensions is based on two questions. Great care was taken in the selection of the questions used as inputs, and we will explain as we go how the items were crafted and what they reveal. Respondents placed themselves on a 10-point scale for each item or question; accordingly, for each dimension, we'll report on combined ratings from the two items.

We will also focus on the percentage of people who are considered "flourishing" for each dimension—meaning that, when given an opportunity to rate their well-being on a scale of zero to 10, they gave themselves a high score of nine or 10 for both inputs for that dimension. We will sometimes share flourishing scores where individuals' self-ratings in each of the five areas are scored out of 100 points.

That's the context of ChurchPulse and Barna's assessment of flourishing. It's also worth noting the context in which the data was collected. A pandemic and other significant upheavals in recent years have altered the way people view the world and their place in it. Many have experienced a mental health crisis, lost jobs or in general faced unprecedented life disruptions by forces beyond their control. Additionally, flourishing in the faith domain has taken on a new shape as gatherings have shifted to add online options, even temporarily, and many congregations have dwindled.

It's important to hold these things in mind as you look at national norms, or as you consider the flourishing of your own congregation. Data are always reflective of a certain time and place and should be interpreted in context. But we don't present this research as a singular study to be referred to just once or a pandemic-era profile of the Church. Rather, these dimensions are meant to be evergreen categories for you to better understand the lives, relationships and faith of U.S. adults and churchgoers. The comprehensive view across decades of Barna research urges these are measures that matter—for everyday ministry, seasons of disruption and long-term use.

In the section that follows, we'll dive deeper into ways to measure how people in your church are flourishing and where to nurture well-being through your ministry and discipleship. If people are flourishing, how can you continue to help them grow and bear fruit individually and as vital members of your faith community? And if they're struggling, what can you do to provide support and opportunities to promote their stability or growth?

Decades of Barna research urge these are measures that matter—for everyday ministry, seasons of disruption and long-term use

At a ministry or organization level, you may see these insights on flourishing as something to build on. What are the opportunities for outreach within your community to invite people into the flourishing life of faithfulness? Are there experts you can partner with to address your congregants' needs, especially in areas like physical or mental well-being where your ministry has limited expertise? What new approaches to ministry programs and preaching will address individuals' deepest desires and needs? Or could these five categories of health refresh the perspective of your existing programs and extend the platform of your own initiatives? Barna's flourishing research or the ChurchPulse assessment need not disturb your well-laid plans, but can rather fortify them.

We expect some leaders will find great symmetry and confirmation in these categories of individual flourishing and the results. These are, after all, core aspects of whole-life discipleship. The ChurchPulse assessment may actually seem like a familiar structure that gives order and a trajectory to some of the many things your church is already focusing on and progressing in.

Wherever you find yourself on the journey of understanding and promoting the flourishing of those in your pews, the data, details and recommendations that follow are designed to help you become an expert in the state of your church. ●

Gain additional exclusive and custom insights from Barna's analysis when you and your church take the ChurchPulse.

The State of Human Flourishing in the U.S.

5 Dimensions of Flourishing People

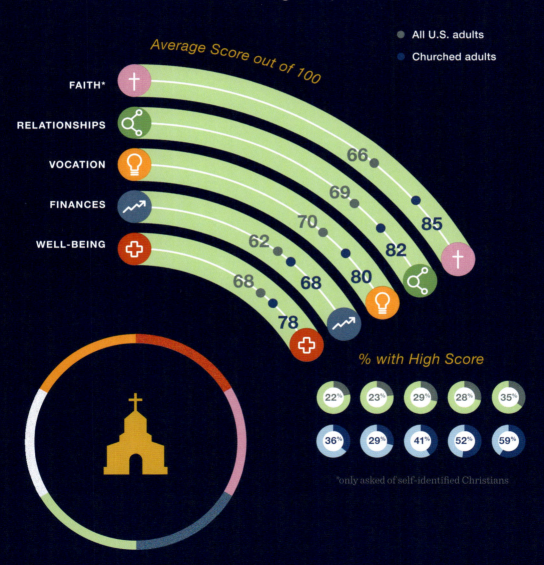

Average Score out of 100

● All U.S. adults
● Churched adults

FAITH*
RELATIONSHIPS
VOCATION
FINANCES
WELL-BEING

66
69
70
62
68
68
80
78
82
85

% with High Score

22% 23% 29% 28% 35%
36% 29% 41% 52% 59%

*only asked of self-identified Christians

Who Tends to Have Higher Scores?

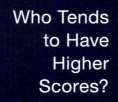

Across the board, flourishing is more common among people who also say they are experiencing a lot of spiritual growth.

Millennials have greater odds of reporting good health, while older generations are stronger in their financial and spiritual well-being. ●

Who Tends to Have Moderate Scores?

Non-practicing Christians consistently lag their practicing Christian peers in measures of flourishing, with the plurality reporting middling scores.

Flourishing has an uneven relationship with education and employment. Adults who have "some"—some college, for instance, or a part-time job—show greater strain than those with more or less education or employment. ●

Who Tends to Have Lower Scores?

People without a spouse or children in the home are less likely than adults with these close relationships to be flourishing.

Churched adults who primarily identify as online viewers have lower flourishing compared to those who are regular in-person attenders, and especially compared to those who are church members. ●

See more data across key demographics in the tables beginning page 108.
n=1,093 U.S. adults, November 11–29, 2019;
n=1,003 churched U.S. adults, September 16–October 4, 2021.

Faith

Measuring faith formation is complicated. We know that at Barna. We bet you, as a faith leader, do too.

The goals of any kind of Christian ministry are multifaceted and, in many ways, can be difficult to capture numerically—especially elements of ministry pertaining to spiritual growth. As we unpack the idea of measuring what matters in our ministries, however, we cannot overlook the *very* important conversation of measuring the flourishing of churchgoers' faith and spirituality. Even secular studies of human flourishing in recent years have flagged religion as a strong predictor of well-being, and the case has been made that religious values and practices must be included in the human flourishing conversation.[10]

In Barna's effort to help churches measure what matters, we have elevated faith to its own dimension of flourishing.

Barna's Historical Study of Christianity

We have dedicated ourselves to the work of attempting to capture the fullest measurement of faith formation possible, striving to understand the intersection of faith and culture in the U.S. and around the world for nearly 40 years.

In this exploration, we have learned that if we *truly* want to measure faith formation and Christian maturation, we have to look beyond affiliation metrics. The vast majority of Americans today still nominally identifies with the Christian faith. In the United States, about seven in 10 adults (68%) call themselves Christians. Though the majority of young and middle-aged adults continues to call themselves Christians, they are less likely than older adults to do so (60% of Gen Z, 68% Millennials, 67% Gen X, 73% Boomers, 72% Elders).

> Religious values and practices must be included in the human flourishing conversation

Over the years, Barna researchers have built various profiles of Christians to more precisely measure faith and gauge commitment and practice in our current cultural moment. For instance, we may report on self-identified Christians but also practicing Christians, evangelicals or "resilient disciples," all of which offer a different lens on Christianity in the U.S.

The study of practicing Christians prioritizes two important elements of Christianity: the practice of regular church attendance and the importance of religious faith

Various Barna Segmentations of U.S. Christians

Self-identified Christian	Practicing Christian	Four-point Evangelical	Resilient Disciple
68 Out of 100	**15** Out of 100	**7** Out of 100	**8** Out of 100

Percentage of U.S. adults who qualify for each faith profile

in one's personal life. Twenty years ago, about four in 10 U.S. adults qualified as practicing Christians. Today, just 15 percent of Americans are practicing Christians. Among those who self-identify as Christian, only about one in four meets these two additional qualifications. Though their numbers are diminishing, their experiences are rich; Barna researchers have found that practicing faith is significantly correlated with higher levels of devotion to the Christian faith, deeper knowledge of the Bible and a hardier commitment to discipleship, faith formation and the pursuit of spiritual flourishing.

Some researchers prioritize measures that capture beliefs rather than practices. For example, the four-point evangelical definition looks for four foundational Christian beliefs—in Jesus as Lord, the Bible's reliability, evangelism and salvation by faith (or, according to David Bebbington's crucicentrism, biblicism, activism and conversionism).[11] Seven percent of adults today meet this evangelical definition. Beliefs may hold more consistent than practices as, over the last 20 years, the percentage of evangelicals according to this definition has only decreased by about 5 points.

In a more holistic effort to measure faith, Barna CEO David Kinnaman has directed recent research toward the resilient disciple. This profile captures a number of beliefs and practices (eight items total), offering a robust picture of the committed churchgoing Christian who wholeheartedly believes foundational Christian doctrine and wants to be "in the world and not of it." This exemplary profile represents 8 percent of U.S. adults. Christians who are resilient disciples are far more likely to commit to the local Church and its people, integrate faith into their day-to-day lives and desire to follow Jesus for a lifetime.

As you can see, if we want to understand modern-day Christianity, there are a number of dimensions and directions of study. For simplicity, accessibility and consistency, Barna focuses on two important items when it comes to our assessment of flourishing.

Commitment to Christ & Commitment to Scripture

Over the years, two elements have remained significant in our research. They play pivotal roles in the profiles mentioned previously and continue to surface in practically all of our research initiatives.

The first item is one's commitment to Christ. Many examples could be selected from Barna's past research to illustrate how one's internal commitment to Christ is a powerful indicator of a flourishing faith. More recently, in Barna's *Growing Together* project, analysts found that uninterrupted time alone with God or purposeful effort to nurture and deepen intimacy with Jesus were accompanied by joy and satisfaction and a sense of being reenergized.[12]

Similarly, over the last 10 years, Barna has remained devoted to studying Bible use and engagement trends through the *State of the Bible* initiative, with American Bible Society. These efforts have given us a view into how one's commitment to scripture is a powerful indicator of human flourishing across *all* of life, but especially for one's faith. Those who are committed to the Bible and revere the role it plays in their lives are significantly more likely to be dependent on God, to share their faith with others and to report experiencing a multitude of personal and communal benefits the Christian faith has to offer.

Faith Flourishing Today

It is in this spirit that the Barna team (alongside analysts representing Gloo, REVEAL, the Christian Life Profile, Prepare-Enrich and other assessment-based organizations) selected two items to capture faith for the ChurchPulse: the centrality of Christ and the centrality of the Bible in one's life.

Why these two? Various "building blocks" of the Christian faith experience overlap. You have probably seen this in your own ministry experience as well: *A Christian who is an active member of a church is likely to also be a Christian who prays often, talks about their faith with others, is dedicated to growing more like Christ through study and relationships, experiences the closeness of God in their daily life*—living a life "wholly devoted to the Lord our God," as 1 Kings 8 instructs. Amid this cluster of inputs that could have all easily been included in the ChurchPulse assessment, our team of analysts found that in today's society, commitment to Christ and commitment to scripture are perhaps the clearest spiritual indicators pointing to a flourishing faith and life.

As of summer 2021, six in 10 churched Christians (59%) are flourishing in the faith dimension, meaning they score a nine or 10 for both of the following statements: *I desire Jesus to be first in my life* and *I believe the Bible has authority over what I say and do.* Younger churched generations are less likely than their elders to have a flourishing faith (42% of Gen Z, 51% Millennials, 62% Gen X, 62% Boomers, 80% Elders), as they show some hesitation to commit to Jesus and scripture.

Churched Christians who attend services weekly are significantly more likely to report having a flourishing faith in comparison to those who attend less frequently (70% vs. 56% who attend monthly, 34% who attend less often).

Worship communities are hubs for developing adults who see Jesus as central and the Bible as influential in their lives— and these qualities are likewise central and influential when it comes to human flourishing. ●

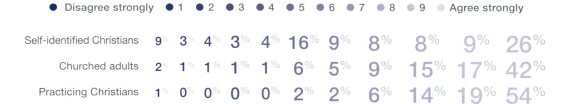

Item 1: "I desire Jesus to be first in my life"

● Disagree strongly ● 1 ● 2 ● 3 ● 4 ● 5 ● 6 ● 7 ● 8 ● 9 ● Agree strongly

	1	2	3	4	5	6	7	8	9	Agree strongly
Self-identified Christians	5%	2%	1%	3%	2%	14%	7%	9%	9%	10%	39%
Churched adults	1%	0%	0%	1%	1%	4%	5%	9%	13%	12%	55%
Practicing Christians	0%	0%	0%	0%	0%	1%	1%	5%	10%	12%	72%

Item 1: "I believe the Bible has authority over what I say and do"

● Disagree strongly ● 1 ● 2 ● 3 ● 4 ● 5 ● 6 ● 7 ● 8 ● 9 ● Agree strongly

	1	2	3	4	5	6	7	8	9	Agree strongly
Self-identified Christians	9%	3%	4%	3%	4%	16%	9%	8%	8%	9%	26%
Churched adults	2%	1%	1%	1%	1%	6%	5%	9%	15%	17%	42%
Practicing Christians	1%	0%	0%	0%	0%	2%	2%	6%	14%	19%	54%

High Faith Flourishing (scores 9 or 10 on individual items)

● Self-identified Christians ● Churched adults ● Practicing Christians

	Self-identified Christians	Churched adults	Practicing Christians
Item 1	49%	67	83%
Item 2	35%	59%	73%
Faith flourishing (combined 1 & 2)	35%	59%	75%

n=722 U.S. Christian adults, April 28–May 5, 2020;
n=1,003 U.S. churched adults, September 16–October 4, 2021.

Relationships

We are living in the most "connected" era in human history. Yet the obstacles to authentic, meaningful relationships are many.

In Barna's 2019 global study of 18–35-year-olds—appropriately called *The Connected Generation*—we found that 77 percent of young adults in 25 countries say events around the world matter to them. More than half sense a connection to people around the world.[13] This is likely nurtured by digital access, social media, globalization and younger generations placing a great value on community.

At the same time, only one-third of 18–35-year-olds often feels deeply cared for by those around them or feels that someone believes in them. Some young adults—especially those who are unemployed, students, women, unmarried or anxious—encounter feelings of loneliness.

This paradox of being connected-yet-disconnected is pronounced among Millennials and Gen Z and no doubt relates to technology—teens and young adults are quick to recognize how devices separate them from others. Relational burdens, however, are not unique either to younger generations or to a digital era. In a 2019 Barna study, anxiety (42% U.S. adults, 37% practicing Christians), depression (39%, 33%) and loneliness (32%, 29%) surfaced as the primary challenges

to relationships and were consistent inside and outside the Church.[14]

After the onset of the pandemic, social distancing only compounded modern conditions for isolation. In the winter of 2020, according to Barna research conducted with Susan Mettes for her book *The Loneliness Epidemic*, about one in six people who attend church regularly (16%) said they were lonely all the time. A majority was lonely at some point in any week.[15]

Barna's research over the years has flagged these and other challenges to relationships—as well as the benefit of being in community, especially when it includes a church.

The Blessings of Relationships

It's important for pastors to take note of how relationships are integral not only in well-being but in discipleship and faith formation.

For instance, in a 2018 study of U.S. households, we observed that hospitality is correlated with an increase in spiritual activity.[16] Households that regularly hosted nonfamily guests were more likely to come together to talk about faith, pray or read the Bible. Interestingly, these homes also witnessed an increase in other less explicitly spiritual activities like shared hobbies, deep conversations or recreational interactions. Households that prioritized faith generally prioritized togetherness, and these values permeated their routines.

Relationships are integral not only in well-being but in discipleship and faith formation

David Kinnaman and his *Faith for Exiles* co-author Mark Matlock also found that meaningful relationships within the Church are a crucial ingredient in being a "resilient disciple."[17] The overwhelming majority of young adults who meet this definition says church is a place where they belong, that someone encourages them to grow spiritually and that they are connected to a community of Christians. These ties aren't new, either; typically, resilient disciples admire the faith of their parents and had close friendships with adult churchgoers in their growing-up years.

At any age, churchgoers may have their life and faith changed by the people they get to know in lobbies, sanctuaries, Zoom rooms or small groups.

Relational Flourishing Today

So, we've learned that relationships are keys in connection, in faith—and, further, we've learned that relational flourishing plays a significant role in human flourishing overall. In fact, regression analysis showed that this variable has a strong relationship with life satisfaction when controlling for the effects of other variables.

What is the state of relationships in the U.S. Church today?

As of summer 2021, overall, churched adults fare better than the general population in their relationships, though they are still split in their relational flourishing. Just over half (52%) are strong in this dimension (vs. 28% of the general population). Fifty-four percent score highly (nine or 10) in their relational satisfaction and 58 percent score highly in their relational contentment, the two items assessed by the Church Pulse. For practicing Christians, the percentage with a high relational flourishing score overall ticks up to 61.

As you might expect, close family helps to foster relational flourishing. Churched adults with spouses or young children see a boost in reported contentment and satisfaction in relationships (58% with children at home and 61% who are married have high scores in the relational dimension vs. 49% of those without children at home and 43% of all single churched adults).

The Church's Impact

Consistent church attendance is a factor in relational flourishing, with 60 percent of churched adults who attend weekly having high scores in this category. Other measures of commitment—such as leading in some capacity at a church (61%), staying in a church for a long tenure (58% who have been in a church more than 10 years) and experiencing "a lot" of spiritual growth in the past year (70%)—also hang together with high scores in relational contentment and satisfaction.

Thus, we see that adults who are flourishing relationally commonly report a quality of thriving churches: connected community (see page 78 for more). Among the half of churched adults who score highly in their relational satisfaction and contentment, 68 percent report high scores for their church community, saying they feel connected there and they have church relationships that encourage accountability. By comparison, just one in five churched adults who aren't flourishing relationally experiences this connected community at church.

Relationally flourishing churched adults don't just have connections at church that are meaningful, they also have *many* connections; a slight majority (54%) reports knowing more than 15 people at church well, with one in three (34%) knowing more than 30 well.

This research can't clarify the direction of these trends—that is, whether people who are engaged in church then see improvement in relationships, or if people who are driven by or secure in relationships tend to find their way to church engagement. Likely, it's some combination of both. Other individual factors, like marital status or personality, or church factors, like programs or congregation size, may also be at play.

The bottom line is the same: A rooted church life and a flourishing relational life often go together.

Relating to Relational Needs

Barna research has shown that many practicing Christians report investing most of their relational time and energy into their churches, second only to their families. Their commitment isn't just to listen to a sermon, receive sacraments and pass an offering plate; for many, their commitment is to the people.

Churches can continue to nurture that commitment, perhaps by better addressing areas of relational need and the people who are most likely to face them. For example, across the board, single adults are on the lower end of relational flourishing compared to their married peers. Yet, as of 2019, pastors and priests said they rarely mentioned unwanted singleness in their sermons (37% once a year, 22% never); few even felt equipped to do so (17% "very" equipped).[18]

A church that not only welcomes and connects people but also operates out of an awareness (if not a proficiency in) in the realities of what it takes to be content and satisfied in relationships today is key in supporting the whole-life flourishing of congregants. ●

Item 1: "I am content with my friendships and relationships"

● Disagree strongly ● 1 ● 2 ● 3 ● 4 ● 5 ● 6 ● 7 ● 8 ● 9 ● Agree strongly

	Disagree strongly	1	2	3	4	5	6	7	8	9	Agree strongly
All U.S. adults	2%	1%	2%	3%	3%	16%	8%	14%	16%	12%	22%
Churched adults	1%	0%	1%	1%	2%	4%	5%	9%	17%	18%	40%
Practicing Christians	1%	0%	0%	2%	2%	4%	4%	7%	14%	18%	49%

Item 2: "My relationships are as satisfying as I would want them to be"

● Disagree strongly ● 1 ● 2 ● 3 ● 4 ● 5 ● 6 ● 7 ● 8 ● 9 ● Agree strongly

	Disagree strongly	1	2	3	4	5	6	7	8	9	Agree strongly
All U.S. adults	3%	2%	4%	3%	5%	16%	8%	12%	17%	11%	18%
Churched adults	1%	1%	1%	2%	2%	5%	6%	11%	17%	23%	31%
Practicing Christians	1%	1%	1%	2%	2%	4%	5%	10%	15%	24%	36%

High Relational Flourishing (scores 9 or 10 on individual items)

● All U.S. adults ● Churched adults ● Practicing Christians

	All U.S. adults	Churched adults	Practicing Christians
Item 1	34%	58%	67%
Item 2	29%	54%	60%
Relational flourishing (combined 1 & 2)	28%	52%	61%

n=1,093 U.S. adults, November 11–29, 2019;
n=1,003 U.S. churched adults, September 16–October 4, 2021.

Vocation

Vocation transcends occupation. This deeper sense of work encompasses what an individual is called to do in the world, and understanding this purpose is an essential part of living a fulfilled and meaningful life. Every person, Christian or not, is seeking the answer to the question "Why am I here?"

Years of Barna research surrounding calling and purpose show having a foundation of faith is largely connected to one's ability to answer this question. To best minister to people, it is essential for pastors to understand how congregants view the interconnectedness of vocation and calling . The Church has a major opportunity to teach congregants what it means to pursue a life of purpose, especially as it relates to vocation.

Pandemic-Era Work / Life Satisfaction

Since the pandemic began, many Americans have seen an increase in the amount of time they spend working each day. This is true despite the supposed flexibility of remote work options and the fact that other parts of the world are simultaneously seeing a decrease in working hours. While many have accrued more hours at a primary job, some have also taken on a second job to supplement income, while working parents are navigating new challenges to hav-

ing sufficient childcare.[19] Accordingly, employed Americans are burning out, hopeful for a better work-life balance and ready to negotiate with—or leave—their employers for something more sustainable.[20]

These shifts are revealing of the vocational longing in working adults. Regardless of their church attendance or Christian affiliation, they tend to agree that being fulfilled is more important than making money. Most working Americans maintain a positive outlook on their careers, with just over four in five (38% agree strongly, 43% agree somewhat) stating they find some level of purpose and meaning in the work they do.[21]

Those with practicing faith have a deeper vocational awareness and satisfaction overall.[22] According to Barna's 2018 report *Christians at Work*, Christians who integrate their faith and their work (just 28 percent of employed Christians) consistently acknowledge God as having a role in the work they do and in their vocation. Nine in 10 (89%) agree strongly that God has given them talents to use for his glory. Two-thirds are strongly aware of these God-given gifts (66%) and clearly see how their work serves God or a higher purpose (66%). Even with this higher-than-average awareness, Christians who integrate their faith and work still seek greater understanding of their calling (40%).

In *Gifted for More*, a 2021 Barna report specifically studying gift awareness, development and generosity among practicing Christians, data show pastors overwhelmingly see people's gifts as reflecting the God who created them (98%). Yet leaders state congregants' giftings are more often celebrated for the difference they make *in* the church (82% agree at least somewhat) than *outside* the church (61%), and they admit there is little structure in the church to support gift development.[23]

> ## The Church has a major opportunity to teach congregants what it means to pursue a life of purpose

Congregants are eager to use their gifts purposefully, to do more with their occupation than pay the bills. It is essential that pastors understand how a person's faith fuels their calling, and help congregants strengthen this bond.

Care for Younger Generations

Vocation should be a topic of discussion at every adult life stage, not just for those in the middle of their careers. For younger generations, vocational development / discipleship is especially key, as they are hyperfocused on success and achievement. As reported in Barna's *Gen Z Vol. 2*, nearly all in this generation (91%) say they hope to achieve a great deal in the next decade.[24]

Pressure around academic and professional success weigh heavily on teens and young adults, even as they are just getting started. In research for *You on Purpose*, Barna found that younger generations are less satisfied and more frustrated than older generations about work. For instance, three in five Gen Z adults (61%) feel stressed about work (compared to 48% of Millennials, 47% of Gen X and 42% of Boomers).[25]

This highlights an opportunity for church leaders to help relieve some of the pressure younger generations are feeling around vocation and calling, as well as communicate the everyday relevance of faith to an already skeptical generation.

Vocational Flourishing Today

Two in five churched adults (41%) have high scores (nine or 10) in vocational flourishing, agreeing that their lives' endeavors are worthwhile and that they understand their purpose in life.

Faith practice, commitment to a church and spiritual growth definitely play a role in vocational flourishing. Practicing Christians fare better than non-practicing Christians in this category (50% vs. 23%). Vocational flourishing is also more common among those who attend church weekly

(47%) as compared to those who attend monthly (38%) or less often (31%). Over half of churched adults who have experienced a lot of growth in the last year (57%) are vocationally flourishing, far more than those who have spiritually grown only some (34%) or less (24%).

Demographics highlight some needs in vocational fulfillment. For instance, gaps arise correlated to levels of education (46% college or more vs. 34% some college or trade school), household income (48% $100K or more vs. 34% less than $50K) and employment (44% full-time vs. 33% part-time, 41% unemployed)—the notable decline here occurring among those working *less* rather than not at all.

Stage of life or household may also align with gaps in vocational flourishing, with adults who are married (49% vs. 33% single) and adults who have children in the home (46% vs. 39% without children under 18 in the home) faring better in this area.

As mentioned earlier, age and life experience can affect how one views their vocation, career and gifts. Across the board, data show that the younger one is, the less likely they are to be vocationally flourishing. Elders—typically retired—hold the highest score, with roughly half (54%) flourishing in this dimension. Boomers (45%), Gen X (41%) and Millennials (37%) secure the middle ground here, while just one in three Gen Z (33%) reports flourishing in this area.

The Need for Community

Research has shown that, for the most part, people assume they'll have to journey toward finding their calling by themselves. Barna data from the book *You on Purpose* show over half of U.S. adults (57%) and practicing Christians (56%) believe that understanding one's calling is primarily a solo journey.[26]

Yet we see that when a churched adult feels a sense of deep connection with their church and fellow congregants, they are three times as likely to experience vocational flourishing (66% vs 21% of churched adults who do not have connected community at church).

Barna's research indicates that at least half of U.S. adults (21% definitely, 32% probably) would be interested if their local church addressed vocational well-being in their preaching and programs. Young Americans are particularly open to this idea, with nearly seven in 10 Gen Z (67%) and Millennials (69%) affirming this.[27]

There is a distinct opportunity here for churches to step in and assure people they aren't on their own in their journey toward purpose. Local churches can become places where people find the community they need to process and discern their calling with others and take structured steps toward vocational flourishing. ●

Item 1: Overall, to what extent do you feel the things you do in your life are worthwhile?

● Not at all worthwhile ● 1 ● 2 ● 3 ● 4 ● 5 ● 6 ● 7 ● 8 ● 9 ● Completely worthwhile

	Not at all	1	2	3	4	5	6	7	8	9	Completely
All U.S. adults	2%	1%	2%	2%	4%	14%	8%	13%	19%	14%	21%
Churched adults	1%	0%	1%	1%	2%	7%	7%	11%	22%	20%	29%
Practicing Christians	1%	0%	1%	1%	1%	5%	5%	10%	20%	22%	35%

Item 2: "I understand my purpose in life"

● Disagree strongly ● 1 ● 2 ● 3 ● 4 ● 5 ● 6 ● 7 ● 8 ● 9 ● Agree strongly

	Disagree	1	2	3	4	5	6	7	8	9	Agree
All U.S. adults	5%	2%	3%	3%	2%	17%	8%	11%	17%	12%	21%
Churched adults	1%	1%	1%	2%	2%	7%	7%	13%	19%	16%	31%
Practicing Christians	2%	0%	1%	1%	1%	6%	6%	9%	20%	17%	37%

High Vocational Flourishing (scores 9 or 10 on individual items)

● All U.S. adults   ● Churched adults   ● Practicing Christians

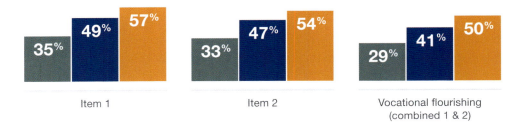

	Item 1	Item 2	Vocational flourishing (combined 1 & 2)
All U.S. adults	35%	33%	29%
Churched adults	49%	47%	41%
Practicing Christians	57%	54%	50%

n=1,093 U.S. adults, November 11–29, 2019; *n*=1,003 U.S. churched adults, September 16–October 4, 2021.

Finances

Finances relate meaningfully to our ability to navigate the world and how we see ourselves or our future. Though financial stability is not the only or even the most important factor in human flourishing, look at any study through the lens of income or socioeconomic status, and remarkable differences are likely to emerge. Finances are also a more tangible or practical factor among the dimensions that contribute to human flourishing, as opposed to, say, satisfying relationships or a sense of vocation.

As Americans work to make sense of new economic realities in a pandemic era, and as Barna gives a glimpse of how churched adults are doing in finances, pastors have an invitation to reevaluate how money and stewardship show up in their discipleship efforts.

Financial Flourishing Today

The financial dimension of flourishing doesn't focus on a particular income level or threshold, but instead measures a sense of stability or provision. Such measures include the degree to which one worries about meeting monthly living expenses and whether food, safety or housing emerge as ongoing stressors.

Currently, 29 percent of churched adults are financially flourishing, based on their combined high score (nine or 10) on these two items. These church attendees fare slightly better than the general population. In 2021, Barna research shows 22 percent of churched adults and 25 percent of practicing Christians say they "do not ever worry" about meeting normal monthly living expenses. Comparatively, recent data among all U.S. adults reveal 17 percent have no worries about money to cover monthly obligations.

There are several reasons a churchgoer might be likely to experience more financial stability—faith practice and churchgoing are common among older adults in established phases and stages of life, for instance, and there may be support systems (tangible or intangible) associated with being someone in religious community that also boost a sense of financial stability. We do see, more broadly, there seems to be growing financial stability for Christians overall. Nearly three in five self-identified Christians say, "I am fairly secure, able to make ends meet and I have some money left over each month"—a 20 percent increase since 2016. Likewise, the number of U.S. Christians saying "I need financial help from others to make ends meet" has also decreased by half, from 8 percent in 2016 to 4 percent in 2021.

Let's look at some of the other demographic factors at play.

We consistently see that money and success preoccupy younger generations and are important priorities to them in a season of laying foundations for their life and career. Financial independence is seen as a primary marker of maturity / adulthood among Gen Z. Our surveys of 13–18–year-olds show a strong desire to finish their education, start a career and become financially independent by age 30. For now, however, this drive is contrasted by below-average financial flourishing scores (18% in Gen Z have a high score).

Some of these patterns in age are no doubt confounded with other stages of life. For instance, marital status also advances financial flourishing, with married churched adults more than doubling those who are single / never married in reporting high financial flourishing scores (33% vs. 16%).

Though financial flourishing is not defined by income, it is at least strongly correlated. Perhaps no surprise, we see that the less a person makes, the lower that person's financial flourishing score. Nearly three in five churched adults who make less than $50,000 annually (58%) rank low in financial flourishing, with only one in five (21%) offering a high score. As income increases, the likelihood of having high scores increase (33% of churched adults making $50–99K and 37% making $100K+).

There are, however, limits to looking at financial well-being as an indicator of overall flourishing. Other measures of flourishing are steady or even higher when people have fewer resources. For instance, in American Bible Society's 2021 *State of the Bible* report, written in collaboration with Barna, scripture engagement and church engagement were more significant predictors of holistic well-being than factors like finances.[28] These individuals may recognize that their needs exceed earthly resources—that "this same God who takes care of me will supply all your needs from his glorious riches" (Philippians 4:19).

Formation & Financial Flourishing

This brings us back to the role of the Church.

Most pastors (80%) agree there is a difference between financial stability and financial flourishing. They're also aware of the discipleship needs surrounding money as many Christians struggle to connect their spiritual life to financial decisions.[29]

When we use the word "flourishing" in the church, we are describing a congregation experiencing a fullness of life marked by, among other things, spiritual maturity, community and overall well-being. Flourishing may mean numerical or financial growth—or it may not. In fact, it could mean intentional focus with limited resources.

Churches can help congregants see how the gospel practically speaks to financial responsibility. Barna data reveal many Christians have the ability and willingness to be generous, both in how they give and serve others. If financial well-being is strong or growing in your church, congregants could also adopt the idea of shared financial flourishing—helping their neighbor flourish as well. ●

Item 1: How often do you worry about being able to meet normal monthly living expenses?

● Worry all of the time ● 1 ● 2 ● 3 ● 4 ● 5 ● 6 ● 7 ● 8 ● 9 ● Do not ever worry

	1	2	3	4	5	6	7	8	9	Do not ever worry
All U.S. adults	5%	2%	5%	6%	5%	17%	7%	11%	12%	9%	17%
Churched adults	6%	3%	4%	4%	4%	9%	8%	12%	16%	11%	22%
Practicing Christians	7%	3%	4%	5%	4%	8%	6%	10%	17%	12%	25%

Item 2: How often do you worry about safety, food or housing?

● Worry all of the time ● 1 ● 2 ● 3 ● 4 ● 5 ● 6 ● 7 ● 8 ● 9 ● Do not ever worry

	1	2	3	4	5	6	7	8	9	Do not ever worry
All U.S. adults	5%	3%	3%	5%	6%	18%	8%	10%	12%	11%	19%
Churched adults	6%	2%	3%	4%	5%	9%	8%	13%	14%	12%	25%
Practicing Christians	5%	2%	3%	4%	5%	8%	6%	10%	15%	12%	30%

High Financial Flourishing (scores 9 or 10 on individual items)

● All U.S. adults ● Churched adults ● Practicing Christians

	All U.S. adults	Churched adults	Practicing Christians
Item 1	26%	33%	37%
Item 2	30%	36%	42%
Financial flourishing (combined 1 & 2)	23%	29%	35%

n=1,093 U.S. adults, November 11–29, 2019;
n=1,003 U.S. churched adults, September 16–October 4, 2021.

Well-Being

Emotional, mental and physical health are interconnected; where one increases, it is likely the others will increase as well. These patterns aren't new, and, especially in a pandemic era, they are essential intersections for today's churches to examine and learn how to navigate. A primary goal of measuring what matters in your church community is to understand how to attend to the needs of congregants and respond well to struggle and suffering among members.

The Need for Mental & Emotional Support

Barna's extensive research focused on the next generation has naturally led to exploration of anxiety's acute presence in society. U.S. teens often tell Barna they are discouraged about the future (46%), lonely (44%) and full of dread or fear (36%) at least some of the time.[30] This isn't unique to the U.S. In a global Barna study of young adults ages 18–35, two in five were anxious about important decisions, uncertain about the future and afraid to fail (40% each). Another three in 10 (28%) were sad or depressed, while nearly one-quarter (23%) felt lonely and isolated from others.[31] Analysts see a twofold interpretation here: We can attribute the prevalence of anxiety to the strain felt by younger generations, but

also to their increasing cultural openness to acknowledging mental health problems in the first place.

Still, perceptions of mental health and how to support it differ inside and outside the Church. For instance, a 2018 Barna study found that Christians, especially practicing Christians, are less likely than non-Christians to have sought treatment for mental illness from a counselor. We also learned that when therapy is sought out, it is rarely because of a pastor's recommendation.[32] These trends may reflect Christians experiencing either greater confidence in their mental health or heightened reluctance to broach the subject in their circles.

Overall, Christians are warm to a mix of spiritual and psychological tools for addressing mental and emotional challenges. Consider that, in Barna's 2020 study on *Restoring Relationships*, practicing Christians were more likely than the general population to say that counseling should be a part of healing in relationships, as well as more likely to see personal faith as the solution to mental health problems.[33]

Though spiritual and scriptural guidance is the primary domain of the church, leaders who dismiss or only superficially address the importance of well-being risk missing a key dimension of discipleship—

especially for younger generations who are already wondering if faith is relevant to their daily lives. Barna's research suggests that, in the local church, this conversation is only going to grow over time. In the fall of 2021, three in four pastors agreed that the mental health of their congregation has become a more important issue for their church to address.[34] Through careful teaching, credible partnerships and compassionate prayer, churches have the opportunity to broaden perspectives and holistically care for people mentally and emotionally.

Well-Being Today

Half of all churched adults Barna surveyed (51%) score high (nine or 10) in their overall mental health (compared to 34% of the general population). As far as physical well-being is concerned, over one-third of churched adults (36%) rates their health highly (compared to 22% of the general population). Some demographic groups fare better, or at least report doing so. Across both physical and mental health scores, it seems men, individuals with children in the home, married adults, adults with a college education, full-time workers and high earners feel stronger. Being involved in a church community also relates to greater flourishing in one's mental and physical health.

We'll reiterate the caveat that human flourishing, and health in particular, is especially tricky to observe solely through self-reporting. Conceptions of personal physical health are often broad; some might consider not actively having a critical condition as being in excellent health, while others may consider having a mild condition as being reason to rate themselves as having poor physical health. It's important to contextualize these measures of well-being, which is best done by looking to multiple sources and experts— something we'd recommend ministries do as they care for congregants and aim to better understand the state of their physical and mental well-being.

Leaders who dismiss or only superficially address the importance of well-being risk missing a key dimension of discipleship

Objectively and globally, we know recent years have brought on severe physical health challenges and burdened healthcare systems. At the time of this writing, more than 840,000 COVID-19 deaths have been recorded in the U.S. alone, with many more having been affected by the virus and some experiencing mysterious "long COVID" symptoms.[35]

A brighter light is now shining on the complicated interplay being physical and mental well-being.

Long before the current public health crisis, researchers were studying the impact of loneliness or isolation, what some call "the shadow epidemic," and how they affect one's physical health. A 2015 study conducted by Brigham Young University professors Julianne Holt-Lunstad and Timothy B. Smith even uncovered a link between loneliness and mortality.[36] Through COVID-19 and the resulting periods of lockdown and social distancing, a loneliness epidemic and a viral pandemic converged. A Harvard study conducted in late 2020 noted a drastic increase in loneliness since the onset of the pandemic, highlighting that one in three Americans (36%) reported experiencing serious loneliness—feeling lonely "frequently" or "almost all the time or all the time."[37] Young adults and mothers of young children are most likely to be affected by serious loneliness. Recent data from Pew Research Center also show about one-third of Americans reporting at least 3–4 sleepless nights each week.[38]

The church's role in ministering to these needs is both crucial and increasingly complicated. In his book *The Resilient Pastor*, Glenn Packiam describes how pastors' uphill climb to regain public credibility has grown steeper during the pandemic, as clergy have had responsibility to minister through a health crisis and make decisions for the collective amid polarized ideas about safety.[39]

While communities may not look to churches for treating physical or mental health, they do look to churches to answer scripture's call to love neighbors, to care for the downtrodden or the "least of these" and to seek out and bring healing to those who are sick and in need, as Jesus did in his earthly ministry. In the research, too, it is clear churches are a witness to if not a contributing factor in well-being. Past and recent studies show that U.S. adults who are plugged into congregations fare better than those who do not, and there are multiple reasons worship communities might provide psychological, social, financial and health benefits to participants, directly or indirectly.

We encourage churches to see this dimension of human flourishing not as a scorecard for how congregants are doing and where they can improve, but as an indicator of areas where ministries can do the sacred work of coming alongside those facing pain, illness, trauma or grief. From pointing to professional mental health resources to considering the safety and accessibility of gatherings, from visiting hospital bedsides to allocating funds to help those who are vulnerable get treatment, local churches can act as safe havens and support systems for churchgoers—in their spirits, souls and bodies. ●

Item 1: In general, how would you rate your physical health?

● Poor ● 1 ● 2 ● 3 ● 4 ● 5 ● 6 ● 7 ● 8 ● 9 ● Excellent

	1	2	3	4	5	6	7	8	9	Excellent
All U.S. adults	2%	1%	3%	5%	6%	15%	11%	15%	20%	10%	12%
Churched adults	1%	0%	1%	2%	3%	8%	8%	17%	24%	17%	19%
Practicing Christians	2%	0%	1%	2%	3%	8%	7%	17%	25%	17%	19%

Item 2: In general, how would you rate your mental health?

● Poor ● 1 ● 2 ● 3 ● 4 ● 5 ● 6 ● 7 ● 8 ● 9 ● Excellent

	1	2	3	4	5	6	7	8	9	Excellent
All U.S. adults	3%	2%	3%	4%	5%	13%	8%	10%	18%	15%	19%
Churched adults	1%	1%	1%	2%	3%	6%	6%	12%	19%	21%	30%
Practicing Christians	1%	1%	1%	1%	2%	4%	5%	11%	18%	23%	34%

High Well-Being (scores 9 or 10 on individual items)

● All U.S. adults ● Churched adults ● Practicing Christians

	Item 1	Item 2	Well-Being (combined 1 & 2)
All U.S. adults	22%	34%	22%
Churched adults	36%	51%	36%
Practicing Christians	35%	57%	39%

n=1,093 U.S. adults, November 11–29, 2019;
n=1,003 U.S. churched adults, September 16–October 4, 2021.

THE ULTIMATE AIM: ETERNAL FLOURISHING

A Q&A WITH TYLER VANDERWEELE, PH.D.

Professor of epidemiology and director of the Human Flourishing Program at Harvard University

Q: In your work, you have observed significant correlations between attendance of religious services and boosts in aspects of well-being. What does this mean for clergy?

A: Religious participation is strongly associated with numerous health and well-being outcomes including greater longevity, less depression, less suicide, less smoking, less substance abuse, better cancer and cardiovascular disease survival, less divorce, greater social support, greater meaning and purpose in life, greater life satisfaction, more charitable giving, more volunteering and greater civic engagement.

Some of our more recent work has examined online service attendance and suggests much smaller effect. With the restriction on service attendance in certain areas, there should thus be genuine concern that this will adversely affect well-being. Pastors and priests need to encourage in-person community gathering once again post-pandemic. This is important for spiritual well-being itself, but also contributes to a host of other outcomes. The research might be viewed as a callback or an invitation back to community religious life. Where else today do we find a community with the possibility of a shared moral and spiritual vision, a sense of accountability, wherein the central task of the members is to love and care for one another? The combination of the teachings, the relationships, the spiritual practices—over time, week after week, taken together—gradually alters behavior, creates meaning, alleviates loneliness, shapes a person and improves well-being in ways too numerous to fully document.

Q: Barna is seeing that church leaders' own well-being has declined. Any insight or encouragement for this group?

A: Many of the well-being practices that our research and the research of others have uncovered can be helpful, practices such as gratitude, forgiveness, loving acts of kindness and prayer and contemplation. However, challenges will likely remain. These challenges themselves can sometimes be opportunities for growth through suffering. I think it helps to keep in mind the ultimate aim of all of the various activities and efforts of church leaders: It is to improve spiritual well-being; it is to promote eternal flourishing. Although this has been an especially difficult time, focus on that ultimate end. That final purpose can bring considerable meaning and help sustain and even grow oneself through times of difficulty. ●

WHEN PASTORS
FLOURISH

A Q&A WITH JENNI CLAYVILLE

Campus pastor at National Community Church in Washington, DC

Q: What does "flourishing" mean to you?

A: I think people who don't know Jesus enjoy life. But for those of us who do know him, flourishing absolutely includes him. Without him, there is no growth, there is no hope, there is no "next thing" or what we're called to do or called to be. It requires the presence of Jesus to [truly] flourish.

So often people think flourishing is success, but it's not the same thing. Years of history [taught us] to "pull yourself up by the bootstraps and survive." But I think we're seeing that's just not what flourishing looks like anymore.

We must be aware and take time to observe and listen, to hear what God is telling us that we need in this season. We're in a time of God calling us back to him, and if we don't listen, I don't think we will flourish.

Q: What about pastors—how do they flourish?

A: Most pastors, we don't take care of ourselves. We are called to care for others. We're called to bring people to the Kingdom. So, there's some sort of a "Superman mentality" in us that puts [our own health] to the side. The burnout numbers are high. If we don't care for ourselves and pastors are not flourishing, there's no way anyone else is going to flourish. We've got to start from the inside, and it's going to pour out of us.

Q: What is your prayer for church leaders in this season?

A: Rest. Often, we as pastors, as church leaders, get so caught up in the things that have to get done. But have we looked at our families? Have we looked at our spouses? Have we looked at our team members—how are they doing? We are carrying the weight of what's been going on through the pandemic, plus whatever trauma from beforehand. Then, stack that with others who come to [leaders] looking for pastoral care.

Pause and look at your team. How are they doing? Are they thriving or are they surviving? Because surviving is not what we want. We want people who are excited about the Kingdom of God. We want people who are excited to introduce people to community and fight for justice and fight for goodness. ●

SCAN ME

Jenni Clayville offers encouragement to ministry leaders in this season.

A FRESH TAKE ON VOCATIONAL DISCIPLESHIP

A Q&A WITH NICHOLAS PEARCE

Professor, pastor and author of *The Purpose Path: A Guide to Pursuing Your Authentic Life's Work*

Q: Explain what you call "vocational courage." How is this important to overall flourishing?

A: Vocation comes from a Latin word meaning *calling*. So, to understand vocation, we must contend with the fact that we have a *caller*. Vocational courage is having the clarity from God, our caller, to understand what one's life's work and calling is. Then, having the courage or commitment to make difficult choices that are necessary to connect one's soul with one's role. It's having clarity on what the Lord would have you to do and being willing to make tough choices, scary choices, sometimes absurd choices, to align your daily work with your life's work.

Q: How can the Church come alongside people to help them build that courage?

A: Many churches disciple and build community around shared interest, affinity or demographic. Women's ministry, men's ministry, 30-somethings ministry and so on. I think there's opportunity to organize people around vocation and build professional communities for discipleship. Not asking people to surrender their professional identity when they walk in the door but giving them the chance to embrace that as part of God's call and claim on their life. Educators, public servants, police, firefighters, people in medicine—can you imagine if your church had an industry-based discipleship model where people are being discipled intergenerationally impact their chosen areas of endeavor? Now you're able to build relationships and facilitate the flourishing of your membership.

Q: What advice would you give to those having difficulty connecting their work to purpose or feeling passionate about the work they do?

A: As a minister, I am regularly confused and astonished by why God would use me to convey the most beautiful, great message of the gospel of Jesus Christ to reach the human heart when he could just do it himself, without the frailty and fragility of the human vessel. Yet it pleases God to do this. Part of [finding purpose and passion] is recognizing God invites us to partner with him. He enlists us, deploys us as an army on the earth. And God's not just using us to do church work. God is forming us in the process. Work is part of God's call and claim on our lives, but it's not the entirety of it. ●

NURTURING NECESSARY CONNECTIONS

A Q&A WITH ASHLEY WILCOX

Quaker minister, author of *The Women's Lectionary* and founder of *Preaching with Confidence*

Q: How can churches nurture connections with specific groups with a lower rate of flourishing?

A: Look within to ask questions. Why do you want to help these groups? Are they part of your church community or your larger local community? Do you really want to help them? These can be challenging questions, but it's important to have clarity before you start. [Find] organizations that are already doing the work. They have the experience and expertise. It's also important to ask people from these groups what they need. Often, churches [start efforts] without talking to the people they want to help. Ask them what they need, and really listen to the answers.

Q: How can leaders be attuned to the intangible aspects of ministry?

A: [It's important to recognize] the gifts in your congregation. This is a way for people to feel seen and heard. It also helps the pastor build up strong leadership. If a church has a practice of naming gifts in the congregation, people can be challenged to use their gifts.

So much of pastoral work is one-on-one. You're with someone when they're grieving. You're talking to someone who's considering a call to ministry or visiting someone in the hospital. These things are intangible. Remember that one-on-one connection and take joy in the process.

Q: What advice would you offer to pastors for effective preaching in trying times?

A: Part of it is knowing your context, knowing your people and being very clear about what they can and can't handle. If you have a congregation with people who are really suffering, then trying to challenge them more may not be the answer. But if you're in a place where people are in pretty good shape, they may welcome [that push]. Talk about hope for the future. People are really looking for that. We're seeing so much burnout in pastors and others. Doing what's needed to take care of yourself and encourage your community to take care of themselves [is important]. ●

MENTAL HEALTH AND **THE CHURCH**

A Q&A WITH TARA BETH LEACH

Author, pastor of servant ministry & missional life at Christ Church in Oak Brook, Illinois

Q: You're passionate about mental health. Why is this a topic that needs to be addressed in church?

A: We all have mental health. It's just a matter of if or when we will have some sort of disruption that could lead to depression or anxiety. And we know that loneliness, depression and anxiety have been a problem, and that it's on the rise in the midst of the pandemic.

At a very local level, within our own congregation, we have seen suicides in the local high schools. It is an epidemic, as some are saying. And the Church doesn't always do a great job with talking about emotional and mental health. There's this stigma wrapped around it. [In my church, I've been able to say], "I'm not a psychologist, I'm not an expert, but I am a pastor. And I believe the Bible has something to say about this."

Q: What advice would you offer church leaders when discussing mental health?

A: One of the dangerous things we can do is make it seem like there's an easy fix. There are not three easy steps to overcoming depression or anxiety. It is incredibly complex. We see a lot of very well-meaning Christians respond to someone who's suffering with [unhelpful] answers like, "God will never give you more than what you can handle." Anyone who's suffering, it *is* more than they can handle. Invite people into the complexity so that they can see there's no easy fix. Also, create a safer environment so people can come out of hiding to tell their stories.

Q: How can the Church be uniquely equipped to address the broad spectrum of needs we see today?

A: The Church is unique in that we have a hope that the world simply cannot offer. Within that hope, we offer an alternative way of living, engaging and viewing all of the societal aches.

One of the ways we can uniquely be equipped is a simple practice of listening and examining. We talk about the prayer of examination, [asking] the Lord to search [us] and expose where [we've] fallen short. I think the Church could practice a corporate examination by asking, "In what ways have we harmed our brother or sister? In what ways have we harmed our community? In what ways has our witness diminished?" If the Church could learn the corporate practice of examining, out of that lament and confession, we would be more equipped to engage the world. ●

Tara Beth Leach offers more tips for teaching on mental health.

SCAN ME

HELPING WOMEN FLOURISH

A Q&A WITH KADI COLE

Author of *Developing Female Leaders* and *Find Your Leadership Voice in 90 Days*

Q: Based on your research, what's often missing or overlooked in the Church when it comes to serving and creating opportunities for women?

A: One of the key findings from our research is known as the "sticky floor." You've heard of the "glass ceiling"—those invisible barriers in our systems and structures that prevent women from advancing in leadership. But the sticky floor [includes] the thoughts and conversations women have *with themselves* that keep their feet "stuck" to the leadership floor.

For example, in one study we found that men and women apply for new leadership opportunities differently. When a man looks at a job description, if he feels confident about 60 percent of the role, he'll apply for the job and usually assumes he will get it. A woman, on the other hand, needs to feel about 100-percent confident of what's on the job description or *she won't even apply for the job*. Think about that. Even if you are actively advertising an open role in your church, you could have several qualified female candidates who aren't going to apply because they are being too hard on themselves about what you are expecting.

Have some conversations with the women you see with leadership abilities. Help them understand your actual expectations of the job you are recruiting for, explain that you'll train them and invite them to apply. We also found that the longer a woman serves in a church, the stickier her floor tends to get. So, take the effort to recruit even those women who you know well and might assume are confident about their leadership. Let's not let the sticky floor keep any more leaders from thriving within your church.

Q: How can pastors be more intentional to help women in their congregations feel a sense of purpose and fulfillment?

A: First, clearly articulate your church's theology around female leadership. Most leaders would be shocked to know how much energy is wasted by both male and female leaders trying to figure out where she is allowed to lead.

Second, utilize a spiritual gifts assessment to help place women (and men) in volunteer and staff roles that fit their gifts and abilities. The goal is not to help women *feel* a sense of purpose, but to help them *fulfill* their purpose.

Third, make sure you include female Bible characters in your sermons throughout the year. The Virgin Mary at Christmastime and Proverbs 31 on Mother's Day is not enough. ●

PERSPECTIVE FOR
THE FUTURE

A Q&A WITH SCOTT SAULS

Senior pastor of Christ Presbyterian Church in Nashville, author of *A Gentle Answer*, *Irresistible Faith* and other books

Q: What do you think is ahead for vocational ministry?

A: I think people who are authentically in ministry because they're called to it are going to be better and stronger. [Charles] Spurgeon once said, "If you can imagine yourself doing anything but ministry, then do that." I'm one of those people who can't imagine it. Even in a pandemic, I can't imagine doing something different. That doesn't make me more virtuous. It just confirms a sense of calling. And I think people who are really called are probably going to stick and be stronger as a result of what we've been through. [They'll be] better leaders and probably pay closer attention to their own formation, integrity and resilience. I hope the future is bright.

Q: How have your vision and optimism for the Church been strengthened?

A: [Recent] years have driven us, really forced us into a place of either humility or quitting. I'm taken back to how St. Augustine answered the question, "What are the top three virtues of Christianity?" His answer was, "Humility, humility and humility."

In the American Church, we experience a lot more momentum, a lot more resourcing, a lot more ability to put a shine on things that maybe aren't beautiful. Whereas, in other places around the world, there's just not that ability to form an image and a brand around your ministry. I think the last couple of years have been good, especially for the American Church, to force us into a place of humility. By being forced into that place, a lot of us have discovered that it's actually a good place to be. It's a life-giving place, to get low and to stay low and to watch God do his thing there.

God doesn't work through our pride, through our pomp and splendor or through our carefully cultivated image. He works, and does his best work, through weakness. That's where his power shows up. Moving forward to better, more fruitful ministry [requires realizing] it's his ministry, and we're the messengers. We're not the point. We're the pointers. ●

Scott Sauls shares insight for effective, healthy leadership.

A Field Guide for
Promoting Flourishing

4 Steps Toward Purpose & Vocation

God has given your congregation passions and gifts that are meant to extend beyond the church. Here's what Luke Bobo, director of strategic partnerships for Made to Flourish, told Barna churches can do to support vocational development.

1. "Be aware of the plight of those in your congregation and provide them with what my good friend Denis Haack calls 'the gift of unhurried time,' and listen attentively.

2. "Imagine with congregants what is possible with their responsible action and God's providence and sovereignty. What we imagine often comes to pass at the intersection of human responsibility and God's sovereignty.

3. "Listen for reasons for disruption to education and disconnection from the community, as many times these disruptions are due to poor financial decisions or overt and covert injustices.

4. "Find ways to make resources and education accessible based on the schedule of the disrupted. Loving those disrupted from education and those disconnected from community will move us to lead with compassion."

Remember Your Core Values

"The *data* question also drives a *values* question," Reverend Drew Van Culen of Christ Church (Grosse Pointe, Michigan) notes. "What impact do we want our ministry to have, and then, how do we measure and define success within that impact?"

Here are some questions to keep values in mind and stay on mission as you strive to build a flourishing community:

- What do you want your church to be known for, both within the congregation and your local community?
- Who are you uniquely called to serve? Is this evident in your programs and outreach?
- How can you gather and share heartfelt stories that reflect the values of your church?

DATA IN ACTION:
CLOSING FINANCIAL GAPS

Randy Frazee is lead teaching pastor at Westside Family Church in Lenexa, Kansas. In recent years, the church has used Barna's ChurchPulse assessment to better understand the health of their congregants. After realizing members were struggling most with financial flourishing, the church designed a teaching series on finances. Congregants were also given access to a financial literacy course.

"One of the best ways to serve someone is to take time to listen to them and find out where they are," Frazee explains. "Honor them by designing your ministry priorities and strategies to help them close the gap on their desire to flourish."

Big Problems, Brighter Light

When electricity was invented, the use of light wasn't reinvented; it was simply re-imagined. New technology strengthened how light was already being used. Light-bulbs were placed where the candles used to be. The same can be true when embracing a new framework, technology or assessment as you lead your church. Understanding the flourishing in your church is not about reinventing church purposes and priorities, but rather allowing tools and data to shine brighter light on your work in an evolving reality. You likely already have some candles in place, helping your team examine relationships, vocation, well-being and more in your congregation. Could clear research and new resources illuminate your activities and make you more effective in these spaces?

DATA IN ACTION:
TRAUMA & PASTORAL CARE

Brian Carson is pastor of pastoral care at Pure Heart Church in Glendale, Arizona. Carson sees data as a necessary tool, especially as pastoral care changes to fit today's needs.

"In many ways, congregational care has experienced a permanent shift that will affect many things like hospital visitations and ministering to care facilities. There is a widening gap between those with needs and those able or trained to meet those needs.

"I believe the Church has the greatest resources to deal with the biggest issue facing people: trauma. Leveraging resources and mining data to truly help local congregations adopt and implement a trauma-informed approach to ministry—this must be the lens for the next season of the Church. It needs to shape policy, budget, staffing, creativity and technology if we truly want to provide for the health and well-being of our congregants." ●

Flourishing Is a Team Effort

Previous Barna research shows that most Christians, including practicing Christians, do not have any regular interaction with their lead pastor outside of main services and events. Pastors, volunteers and other leaders need to grow and share responsibility for the relational surface area of their ministry.

How well does your church walk alongside people and build community? How do you check in with and get updates on their lives and well-being? What's happening in members' homes or on their jobs? Who can help gather that context?

"There's got to be an investment in the community, but you've also got to be in the community," pastor John Perez of Faith Temple Church of God in Christ, (Beacon, New York) says. "Are you approachable? Do people see the sincerity in you? Do people see that you follow God and have your own relationship with him? If people see those attributes in you, you will [have impact]."

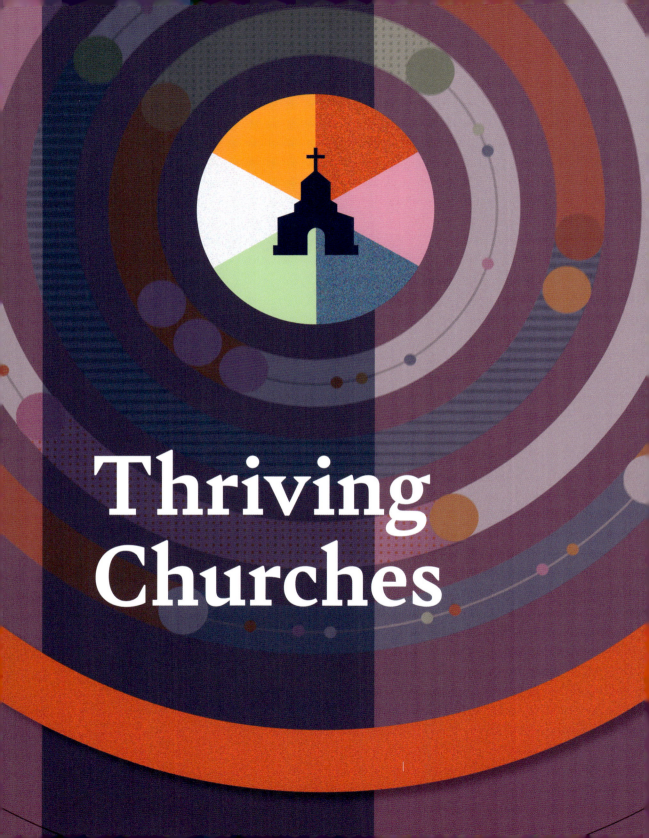

Thriving Churches

FEATURING

- Ed Stetzer
- Nancy Duarte
- Bishop Claude Alexander
- Ryan Burge
- Rev. Dr. Brianna K. Parker
- Mark Chaves

WHY THRIVING CHURCHES MATTER

How healthy and effective is your church?

You may have an intuitive response to this question. Maybe you have anecdotes that demonstrate vitality in your ministry. But do you really know if your congregation is thriving today?

Perhaps you've relied on attendance and giving data to help you track your congregation's overall well-being or growth. These are useful operational metrics, but they fail to tell the real story of whether your church is fulfilling its mission to nurture, send and equip disciples. Many church health consultants and thought leaders today refer to these kinds of metrics as "lagging" indicators, like lights that flash red long after organizational issues or failures have set in.

Additionally, some metrics are less concrete than they once were. You likely don't need us to tell you the ways the pandemic—and the surge of online and hybrid ministry that accompanied it—further complicated the Church's ability to gauge congregational engagement. Even as gatherings resume, churches (and researchers alike) continue to catch up to the shifts, probing how to "count" attendance through online analytics, how to foster community in new contexts, how to keep churchgoers rooted no matter what a service looks like—and how to grow or regain the interest of those whose attendance or membership has lapsed in the pandemic era.

You don't have to figure it out on your own.

Barna, alongside our partners at Gloo, have been building a framework that looks beyond traditional or even numerical indicators of the health of a congregation. More than analyzing historic tracking questions (which have their place in understanding the big picture of Christianity in the U.S. and which Barna has been collecting for decades), we wanted to expand how we measure the state of the Church in this moment—and, now, the state of *your* church. Our exploration of what we call "thriving churches" is rooted in several signs of a ministry's priorities and effectiveness. This framework is available through our Barna ChurchPulse tool, an assessment which allows you to gain a holistic view of your own church environment.

What do we mean by "thriving?" By definition, thriving is vigorous growth. It speaks of a journey toward health and success. Indeed it is a synonym of "flourishing," and it is no stretch to say that the work of promoting human flourishing and building thriving churches is interconnected. Additionally, Barna urges accounting for a pastor's or leader's own flourishing in this equation.

We started by inviting a broad range of leaders, researchers and church consultants to provide input on organizational items that commonly indicate healthy church cultures and systems. Some involve practical or experiential elements of church life. Some involve generosity and relationships. Some involve faith and spiritual disciplines. Some involve more qualitative than quantitative assessment.

Using surveys and statistical modeling, Barna researchers, Gloo analysts and academic advisors studied relationships between thriving factors and variables like human flourishing, life satisfaction and spiritual growth. (You can learn more about this process on page 108.) By using these kinds of analysis "targets," researchers were able to explore organizational thriving beyond numeric growth and church budget alone. Though material indicators are at times significant variables, they are not essential to a thriving church environment. In Barna's beta study, the likelihood of thriving remained consistent across churches of all sizes. *Any* congregation can pursue or experience the qualities of a thriving church.

From an initial survey of 120 questions, a narrow list of 15 key areas or "dimensions" emerged in our analysis. We have grouped them in three categories, moving across the local church—through its congregation, its community and its leadership.

Nurturing
- Worship Experience
- Connected Community
- Prayer Culture
- Bible-Centeredness
- Spiritual Formation
- Trusted Leadership

Sending
- Faith-Sharing
- Serving Others
- Social Impact
- Holistic Stewardship
- Leadership Development

Leading
- Future-Focused
- Resource Stability
- Team Health
- Data-Informed

There are a few ways we'll discuss the results of our nationally representative research on thriving churches. Each of the 15 dimensions is based on two questions. Respondents placed themselves on a 10-point scale for each item or question; accordingly, for each dimension, we'll report on combined ratings from the two items. We will also focus on the percentage of people who are in churches that are considered "thriving" for each dimension—meaning, when given an opportunity to rate their church on a scale of zero to 10, they gave a high score of nine or 10 for both inputs for that dimension.

It's important to note the thriving church research accounts for a spectrum of church sizes, denominations, regions and demographics. There are minimal gaps between responses of mainline and non-mainline Christians. This is rare in our studies of the U.S. Church and shows a remarkable cross-denominational consistency and potential for common ground in the value of these metrics.

As you progress through this section, or as you process your own thriving scores through the ChurchPulse assessment, we'd encourage you to have an incremental approach. Don't try to tackle everything at once. Prayerfully consider what is right or resonant with the vision, mission and context of your church. Our research says these are dimensions to pay close attention to—this is information all church leaders need to know to make decisions; the next steps will be unique to your ministry. What prompts a sense of validation or celebration? Where would you like to pause and learn more? Are there areas where you feel urgency or conviction to improve?

Any congregation can pursue or experience the qualities of a thriving church

Embrace collaboration and conversation as you go, with the voices of your leadership team and perhaps other experts or professionals in your staff or congregation (especially if you don't feel so data-savvy yourself). Be humble, be open to gaining new information—and be strategic, willing to then use that information well.

Adults who are committed to a church do, in fact, often offer higher scores across thriving categories. Still, more than ever, we know that simply counting heads in pews or views on a streaming service cannot fully reveal the impact of a church, the effectiveness of the pastorate or the transformative power of discipleship.

In the pages that follow, you'll find fresh ways to think about all of the above, Sunday through Saturday, and how to measure what matters most in the church you've been entrusted with. ●

The State of Thriving Churches in the U.S.

15 Dimensions of Thriving Churches

● Nuturing ● Sending ● Leading

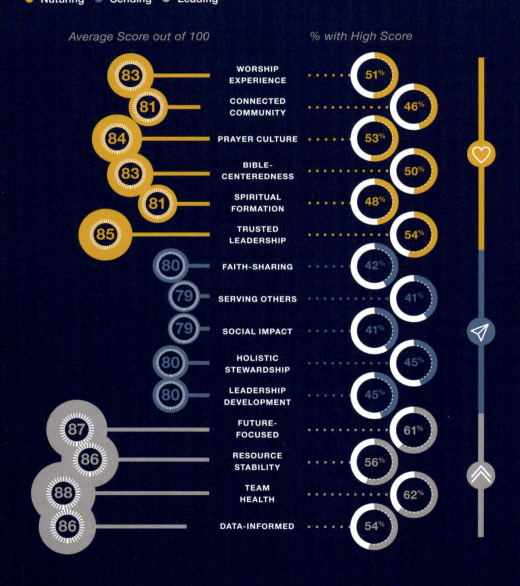

Average Score out of 100 — % with High Score

Dimension	Average Score	% with High Score
WORSHIP EXPERIENCE	83	51%
CONNECTED COMMUNITY	81	46%
PRAYER CULTURE	84	53%
BIBLE-CENTEREDNESS	83	50%
SPIRITUAL FORMATION	81	48%
TRUSTED LEADERSHIP	85	54%
FAITH-SHARING	80	42%
SERVING OTHERS	79	41%
SOCIAL IMPACT	79	41%
HOLISTIC STEWARDSHIP	80	45%
LEADERSHIP DEVELOPMENT	80	45%
FUTURE-FOCUSED	87	61%
RESOURCE STABILITY	86	56%
TEAM HEALTH	88	62%
DATA-INFORMED	86	54%

Routine Thriving

On average, here's how qualities of thriving congregations show up in the schedules and practices of churchgoers.

In the past year …

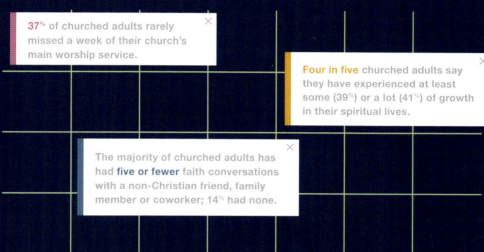

37% of churched adults rarely missed a week of their church's main worship service.

Four in five churched adults say they have experienced at least some (39%) or a lot (41%) of growth in their spiritual lives.

The majority of churched adults has had **five or fewer** faith conversations with a non-Christian friend, family member or coworker; 14% had none.

Each week …

Seven in 10 churched adults pray with others.

39% of churched adults reportedly volunteer in some way at their church.

Nearly three-quarters of churched adults (72%) use their Bible.

10%

16%
23%

Nearly one in four is giving at least 10% of their income to their church; **16%** of churched adults are looking toward giving a traditional tithe amount.

n=1,003 churched U.S. adults, September 16–October 4, 2021.

A THRIVING CHURCH
NURTURES . . .

The first six characteristics of thriving churches that we'll examine are grouped into a category we'll call "nurturing." These dimensions represent the ways that churches cultivate life *within* the congregation—investing in the worship experience, relationships and spiritual development of churchgoers. Ministries that are seeking to build trust with and build up disciples through their regular services, programs and communication should take note. These qualities hang together, offering a holistic depiction of what it means to nurture transformative worship and spiritual growth in a body of believers.

For the most part, we'll be reporting on people who give high scores (nine or 10) for both items in a particular dimension. Some demographic and theolographic groups are more inclined to give high marks, and their positivity is relatively consistent across the thriving categories.

In the shadow of these enthusiastic groups, of course, we find the churched adults who lack strong connections in thriving churches—typically, adults who are single, not raising kids, semi- or unemployed, struggling in their spiritual walk or, for some reason or another, less actively engaged in the life of the church. As you'll see, mention any dimension of thriving, and there's about a 50 / 50 chance that a church has room for at least some, if not drastic, improvement. ●

❯ The Worship Experience

❯ Connected Community

❯ A Prayer Culture

❯ Bible-Centeredness

❯ Spiritual Formation

❯ and Trusted Leadership

Worship Experience

Half of churched adults (51%) give high scores for the worship experience of their church. Specifically, they select a nine or 10 when it comes to feeling closer to God through the main worship service and leaving a service having connected to God or personally experienced God's presence.

Practicing Christians more often report high marks for their connection to God through worship (64%). Similarly, churched adults who are married (55%) or raising children (58%)—groups who tend to be more involved in the life of the church—report higher scores for their church's worship experience than their peers who are unmarried (46%) or who do not have young kids (47%).

Other Barna research points to the things people most value in a weekly worship experience: songs, praying aloud and communion top the list. Churchgoers' preferred worship styles range from traditional (46%) to Spirit-filled (35%).[40] Yet despite variations in liturgy, music and service structure across denominations, there is no significant difference between mainline and non-mainline Christians on the question of connecting with God in worship. This should encourage church leaders that substance may truly transcend style when it comes to thriving in a worship experience. Half of churched adults in both mainline (51%) and non-mainline (52%) congregations report high scores in this area.

A strong worship experience and diligence in church attendance hang together; among churched adults who report high scores for the worship service, nearly half (46%) say they rarely miss a week. ●

Worship Experience
(scores 9 or 10 on individual items)

● Churched adults   ● Practicing Christians

Item 1: "I feel closer to God through the main worship service at this church"

Item 2: "I *always* leave this church's worship service feeling I have connected with God or personally experienced the presence of God"

Worship Experience (combined 1 & 2)

n=1,003 U.S. churched adults, September 16–October 4, 2021.

Connected Community

In a season of profound loneliness, just less than half of churched adults (46% are firmly connected in a faith community, meaning they strongly agree they feel connected and find relationships that encourage accountability in their church. Among practicing Christians, 57 percent report this kind of connected community.

Churched adults in more naturally social life circumstances, such as marriage (52%), parenting (54%) or full-time employment (50%), tend toward giving high scores for connected community. It's also possible these groups benefit from receiving greater emphasis in church programs, teaching or gatherings that focus on the family or household.

The more someone is around or plugged into church life, the more likely they experience it as a strongly connected community. We see this among those who attend weekly (51%), lead in some capacity (54%), have church membership (50%) or have been in their church for more than a decade (51%). Social and spiritual life weave together as well for the churched adults who have experienced a lot of recent spiritual growth (66%) and say they worship in a very connected community.

Though practicing Christians rarely bring "outside" friends in to visit their church, Barna has learned that churched adults regularly hang out with their church friends outside of services (39% weekly). All told, practicing Christians say church is where they invest most of their relational time and energy, second only to family.

Predictably, the possibility of being in a connected community at church increases among those who simply know more people well at their place of worship. ●

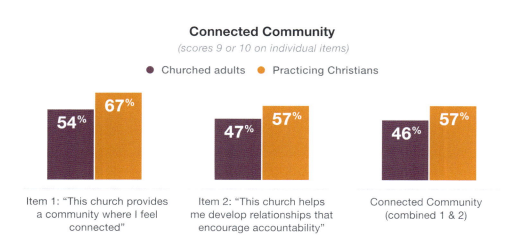

Connected Community

(scores 9 or 10 on individual items)

● Churched adults   ● Practicing Christians

Item 1: "This church provides a community where I feel connected"
54% / 67%

Item 2: "This church helps me develop relationships that encourage accountability"
47% / 57%

Connected Community (combined 1 & 2)
46% / 57%

n=1,003 U.S. churched adults, September 16–October 4, 2021.

Prayer Culture

For the most part, Americans tend to pray silently and by themselves.[41] While corporate prayer may not be a first instinct, more than half of churched adults are seeing the power of this environment.

Fifty-three percent of churched adults offer high scores for the prayer culture of their church. This dimension of thriving accounts for churches where people are developing prayer habits that help to connect with God and seeing the power of prayer through church. More than two-thirds of practicing Christians (67%) strongly agree these are qualities of their church's prayer culture.

Barna has seen that spiritual activities like prayer increase in households with children, and, accordingly, three in five churched adults who are raising kids (61%) experience a thriving prayer culture through their church. Married churched adults score similarly (57%).

These positive reports of witnessing and growing in the power of prayer rise around involvement with church, such as attending regularly (60% who attend weekly), being a church member (59%) or leader (63%) or attending a church long term (59% in a church 10+ years). Engagement in a rich prayer culture also has a natural relationship to seeing spiritual growth (75% who report "a lot" of spiritual growth in the past year).

The frequency and vibrancy of corporate prayer may be tied to each other. Among those who report a strong prayer culture, 37 percent say they pray with others "daily," as opposed to one in five churched adults who gives lower marks for their church's prayer culture (21%). After all, 54 percent of church attendees tell Barna that praying aloud is an important part of their weekly worship experience.[42] ●

Prayer Culture

(scores 9 or 10 on individual items)

● Churched adults ● Practicing Christians

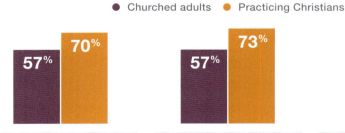

| Item 1: "This church helps me develop habits of prayer that better connect me with God" | Item 2: "I have seen the power of prayer through this church" | Prayer Culture (combined 1 & 2) |

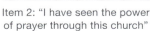

n=1,003 U.S. churched adults, September 16–October 4, 2021.

Bible-Centeredness

Barna, often in partnership with American Bible Society, has long tracked the impact of scripture engagement in the lives of individual Americans, especially practicing Christians. For the congregation at large, too, the Bible is essential to thriving.

Half of churched adults (50%) give a high score to their church for being Bible-centered. Specifically, they think their church does an exceptional job supporting spiritual growth by helping people understand the foundations of the Bible and live out biblical teachings in everyday life. Among practicing Christians, nearly two-thirds (64%) are in a strongly Bible-centered church.

A rare generational gap emerges on this point, with Gen Z being less likely than all older generations to be highly Bible-centered (34% vs. 47% Millennials,

54% Gen X and 53% Boomers). It's possible that Gen Z adults are in a transitional season in church programs and in their faith. Stage of life may be a factor here too, as churched adults who are married (57%) or parents (61%) also have a more Bible-centered experience of their church.

The Bible's centrality is seemingly amplified among those who are more involved with the church, like regular (59% weekly) or long-term (55% 10+ years) attendees, leaders (57%) and members (56%). The more a churched adult is experiencing spiritual growth (70% "a lot" in the past year), the more likely they are to be in a Bible-centered church.

A Bible-centered church includes people who return to the Word often. Two in five churched adults in such an environment (39%) report reading scripture daily. ●

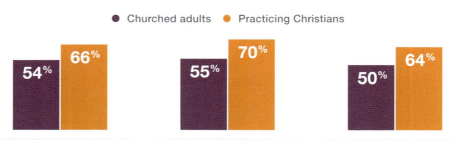

Bible-Centeredness

(scores 9 or 10 on individual items)

● Churched adults ● Practicing Christians

54% **66%**
Item 1: "This church supports my spiritual growth through helping me understand the basic foundations of the Bible *very well*"

55% **70%**
Item 2: "This church helps me live out the teachings of the Bible in my everyday life"

50% **64%**
Bible-Centeredness (combined 1 & 2)

n=1,003 U.S. churched adults, September 16–October 4, 2021.

Spiritual Formation

Strongly related to the aforementioned practices of prayer and scripture study, spiritual formation is another marker of a thriving church, and it's something that 48 percent of churched adults strongly feel is part of their church experience. This means they highly rate their church as a partner in spiritual formation and believe the next steps for their spiritual growth within the church are made clear. For practicing Christians, the percentage that gives a high score for spiritual formation goes up 10 points (58%).

Spiritual formation is seemingly a greater element in some stages of life, including marriage (52%), parenthood (56%) and full-time employment (53%), suggesting congregants who aren't in these seasons may need greater partnership and clarity from their church when it comes to developing their faith.

Church leaders (59%), members (52%) and regular (53% weekly) or long-term (52% 10+ years) attenders are more inclined to praise their church as a partner in spiritual formation.

Unsurprisingly, those who enthusiastically report experiencing spiritual formation in church overlap with those experiencing spiritual growth in their lives (69% of those with a lot of recent spiritual growth report strong spiritual formation in their church; likewise, 60% who strongly agree they are in an environment of spiritual formation report a lot of spiritual growth). Whether their growth draws them into the church or the church draws them toward growth, the effect is to be drawn closer to God. ●

Spiritual Formation

(scores 9 or 10 on individual items)

● Churched adults   ● Practicing Christians

| Item 1: "This church is an essential partner in my spiritual formation" | Item 2: "My next steps for spiritual growth at this church are clear to me" | Spiritual Formation (combined 1 & 2) |

n=1,003 U.S. churched adults, September 16–October 4, 2021.

Trusted Leadership

Thriving churches are stewarded by trusted leaders; 54 percent of churched adults strongly agree this is true in their worship community. This means they have great trust in church leaders and feel communication from the top is clear.

Trust is an area where married adults (57%), parents (60%) and full-time workers (56%) in a congregation are more likely to celebrate their church leadership.

Trust is in short supply, however, among the youngest adult generation. Just 38 percent of churched Gen Z give high marks for trusted leadership in their church, compared to at least half of Millennials (50%), Gen X (57%) and Boomers (54%). It is possible trust will grow with age, but this also reveals an opportunity for honesty and openness with emerging adults. Some ministries may need to address a healthy skepticism among young adults; Barna has seen that younger practicing Christians are more likely than older adults to be affected by a range of church scandals. Thankfully, they tend to feel these incidents were subsequently well-handled, and many stay in church. Still, leaders may have to earn and maintain the trust of younger worshippers who have been exposed to "church hurt."

Naturally, adults who have invested in a church are likely to see it as a body to be trusted. Most weekly attendees, members and tenured churched adults give high scores (61% each). Three-quarters of churched adults experiencing significant spiritual growth (74%) also place great trust in church leadership.

Though it may be an insular view, churched adults who report leading (61%) or being on staff (62%) also give high marks for trust and communication. ●

Trusted Leadership

(scores 9 or 10 on individual items)

● Churched adults   ● Practicing Christians

57%	69%
Item 1: "I have great trust in the leaders of this church"	

60%	73%
Item 2: "Communication from this church is clear"	

54%	67%
Trusted Leadership (combined 1 & 2)	

n=1,003 U.S. churched adults, September 16–October 4, 2021.

A THRIVING CHURCH
SENDS PEOPLE OUT TO . . .

Throughout history and across traditions, giants of the Christian faith have called the Church to look outside of itself—to focus on the people and ministry opportunities found "outside of the four walls," as it is often said.

"What does love look like? It has the hands to help others. It has the feet to hasten to the poor and needy. It has eyes to see misery and want," Saint Augustine said.

Martin Luther King, Jr. applauded the early Church for being "not merely a thermometer that recorded the ideas and principles of popular opinion," but "the thermostat that transformed the mores of society."

More recently, Pope Francis urged, "Instead of being just a Church that welcomes and receives by keeping the doors open, let us try also to be a Church that finds new roads, that is able to step outside itself and go to those who do not attend Mass, to those who have quit or are indifferent."

❯ Share Their Faith

❯ Serve Others

❯ Make a Social Impact

❯ Practice Holistic Stewardship

❯ and Become Leaders

Serving, sharing and making an impact have been pillars of the Christian faith since Jesus modeled this lifestyle in his own ministry. Today, Barna researchers find multiple "sending" activities to be major indicators of church thriving in today's world. Our sending category groups five dimensions related to outward-reaching activities of a church and its people. In summary, a thriving church is one that has successfully launched its people into society to make a difference—as evangelists, servants, workers and change-makers.

Concerningly, scores in this category are some of the lowest across our research on church thriving, elevating the importance of this conversation for pastors today. If you want to lead thriving churches, you cannot neglect these external focuses. Together, let's explore five aspects of sending and aim to better understand how church leaders can develop Christians who "go and make disciples of all nations" (Matthew 28:19), "look after orphans and widows in their distress" (James 1:27) and "let their light shine before others" (Matthew 5:16). ●

Faith-Sharing

Evangelism is central to the activity and growth of the Christian faith. To measure faith-sharing within a congregation, churched adults are asked if their congregation is encouraged to talk about their faith in Jesus with others and equipped to share their faith with the unchurched. About two in five churched adults (42%) offer high scores (nine or 10 on individual items).

Black churched adults are significantly more likely to report feeling very encouraged and equipped by their churches for evangelism (51%). Further, they are having faith conversations with the non-Christians in their lives frequently; 25 percent report 10 or more of these conversations in the last year (vs. 15% of white churched adults, 13% Hispanic, 8% Asian).

Over the past 38 years, Barna has been tracking evangelism trends. The number of Americans who agree strongly that they personally have a responsibility to tell other people about their religious beliefs has dropped from one in three in 2003 to one in five today. In 2019's *Reviving Evangelism* report, Barna researchers uncovered that nearly half of Millennial practicing Christians say it is wrong to evangelize (47%).[43] Many Christians in today's culture seem to have "bubble-wrapped" themselves into Christian circles, hindering opportunities for evangelism; almost two in five practicing Christians say they have no non-Christian friends or family members (38%).

However, those who *have* had at least one conversation about faith came away more confident (86%) and eager to share their faith (71%). Evangelism may also be met with more warmth than some might think—especially among young people! One in three Millennial non-Christians (36%) and almost half of non-Christian Gen Z (47%) say they are interested in learning more about Christianity. ●

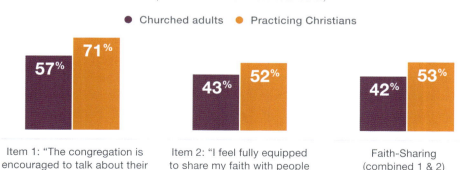

Faith-Sharing

(scores 9 or 10 on individual items)

● Churched adults ● Practicing Christians

71% 57%

Item 1: "The congregation is encouraged to talk about their faith in Jesus with others"

43% 52%

Item 2: "I feel fully equipped to share my faith with people who do not attend church"

42% 53%

Faith-Sharing (combined 1 & 2)

n=1,003 U.S. churched adults, September 16–October 4, 2021.

Serving Others

This dimension measures how a church empowers congregants to make an impact on the lives of others and the extent to which congregants actually take time to serve and help others in the community. Four in 10 churched adults offer high scores (41%). Younger generations feel more empowered by their churches to make a difference and are more likely to prioritize service (44% of Gen Z, 46% Millennials, 47% Gen X vs. 31% Boomers, 34% Elders). Again, we observe that Black churched adults excel in this dimension more so than other ethnic groups (50%).

Barna has devoted significant energy to exploring how Christians can be a more present and welcome influence in their neighborhoods. Just one in five practicing Christians (22%) feels like their gifts and talents are primarily for themselves, while half (54%) understand that their gifts are for "anyone who could benefit from them".[44] Furthermore, the vast majority of practicing Christians agrees that people of faith bear a large responsibility to do good works in the community. How can churches harness this potential and empower and activate congregants to serve their neighbors?

Another important measure of serving others is the health of a church's volunteerism culture. Over the last 20 years, serving others within the Church is a practice that has remained fairly stable; the percentage of Americans who have volunteered to help a church within the last week has dropped fewer than 5 percentage points (23% to 19%). Among churched adults, four in 10 (39%) serve or volunteer at their church weekly. Still, 28 percent don't incorporate church volunteering into their spiritual practices at all. ●

Serving Others

(scores 9 or 10 on individual items)

● Churched adults　● Practicing Christians

Item 1: "I give away my time to serve and help others in my community" — 43% / 49%

Item 2: "This church empowers me to make an impact in the lives of others" — 55% / 66%

Serving Others (combined 1 & 2) — 41% / 49%

n=1,003 U.S. churched adults, September 16–October 4, 2021.

Social Impact

A thriving church might measure social and community impact, specifically through the lens of addressing injustices and helping those who suffer or are marginalized. Forty-one percent of churched adults give high marks for this kind of impact through their church. Black churched adults are the most likely to offer high scores in this area (50% do so).

Boomers are the least likely generation to see this quality in their church (33% vs. 47% of Gen Z, 45% Millennials, 43% Gen X). Generally, though, Barna observes social impact is less of a priority for older adults. Meanwhile, this generational split affirms the trend that young adults are more inclined to desire (or even expect) compassion, community engagement and social impact to be a part of their church experience. Young adults who are meaningfully involved with their faith and church

tend to report that their church has helped them understand the needs of the poor and marginalized and provided opportunities to serve those in need in their community. Their belief and compassionate action hang together and are catalyzed in church community—when one of these slips, the others may as well. For instance, young people often point to human suffering as something that sparks spiritual doubt.[45]

While the majority of pastors says they encourage members to help the poor (69%) or people in distress (73%), only about one-third of practicing Christians ages 18 to 35 says their church has equipped them with an understanding of social justice (35%) or that they've found a cause or issue they're passionate about through their church (31%). How can pastors close this gap and cast a vision for community impact that galvanizes *all* generations in their pews? ●

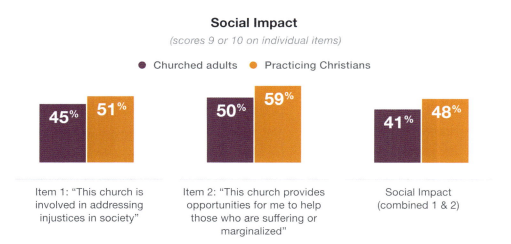

Social Impact

(scores 9 or 10 on individual items)

● Churched adults   ● Practicing Christians

45% 51%
Item 1: "This church is involved in addressing injustices in society"

50% 59%
Item 2: "This church provides opportunities for me to help those who are suffering or marginalized"

41% 48%
Social Impact (combined 1 & 2)

n=1,003 U.S. churched adults, September 16–October 4, 2021.

Holistic Stewardship

As Christians, the ability to use what we've been given for Kingdom purposes is an indicator of a mature faith (see the parable of the talents). Holistic stewardship refers to how well a church is helping congregants embrace their calling and use their gifts and resources to serve God and others. Forty-five percent of churched adults offer high scores for this dimension.

Stewardship is about much more than money or church giving; it applies to skills, time, hospitality, emotional support and other gifts. Indeed, among churched adults, 23 percent of households currently give 10 percent or more to their church (another 16% are working toward giving a traditional tithe, 52% give as they're able and 8% don't give at all). Barna analysts have found, however, a Christian's posture toward whole-life generosity is more important than just their giving tendencies

(although the two do overlap quite a bit).

Encouraging this kind of generous lifestyle is easier said than done; even *understanding* one's gifts is often a struggle for people, and only half of practicing Christians (54%) say they know their own gifts, abilities or skills very well.[46]

Helping congregants find ways to *use* their gifts to honor God is another challenge. Among churched adults who are employed full-time, only half say their church has definitely helped them find ways to use their gifts and embrace their calling (51%). For workers who integrate their faith into their professional work, generosity, integrity and gratification are a package deal.[47] Only 28 percent of Christian workers fit this definition—but closing this discipleship gap offers great reward. Essentially every practicing Christian agrees that as they grow in their gifts, they also grow closer to God (62% strongly, 35% somewhat). ●

Holistic Stewardship

(scores 9 or 10 on individual items)

● Churched adults ● Practicing Christians

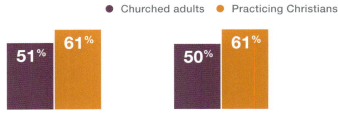

Item 1: "This church helps me find ways to use all of my gifts (time, skills and financial resources) to honor God or serve others"

Item 2: "This church has helped me embrace my calling in life"

Holistic Stewardship (combined 1 & 2)

n=1,003 U.S. churched adults, September 16–October 4, 2021.

Leadership Development

This dimension captures an important element that begins *within* the four walls of a church: developing leaders. Specifically, we'll look at the clarity of leadership training pathways and the degree to which a church empowers young people to become leaders.

Forty-five percent of churched adults give high scores in this dimension. Single congregants are less likely than married adults to see a strong leadership development culture in their church (40% vs. 48%), aligning with previous Barna research that suggests many singles struggle to maintain deep connections within their churches and are often overlooked for leadership opportunities.

Next generation development is a critical predictor not only of church thriving but of church survival. In spite of the "graying" of church leadership, there seems to be an unsettling lack of opportunity for young people to grow in their leadership. Only one in five churched Millennials (21%) says they have access to leadership training for ministry through their church and two in five (42%) say they are given real chances to contribute in their church. But young churchgoers are hungry for opportunities to step up. For example, the majority (72%) expresses a desire to make a difference in the world. As Barna CEO David Kinnaman often says, "Young adults want the church to be a laboratory of leadership, not just a place for spirituality."

Many pastors have voiced difficulty finding men and women who they feel are truly capable of handling leadership responsibilities. However, committing to leadership development is important to build thriving churches that will stand healthy and whole for generations to come. ●

Leadership Development

(scores 9 or 10 on individual items)

● Churched adults   ● Practicing Christians

Item 1: "There is a clear training pathway for developing leaders in this church": Churched adults 48, Practicing Christians 55%

Item 2: "This church empowers young people to become leaders": Churched adults 52%, Practicing Christians 60%

Leadership Development (combined 1 & 2): Churched adults 45%, Practicing Christians 53%

n=1,003 U.S. churched adults, September 16–October 4, 2021.

IN THRIVING CHURCHES, LEADERS . . .

As we bring our reporting about thriving churches to a close, we will focus on activities directly related to leading. The dimensions within this category uniquely offer a peek behind the curtain of church operations, ministry strategy, decision-making and effectiveness.

Due to the nature of the items we are attempting to measure, this set of questions was only asked of churched adults who self-identify as leaders in their churches. Today, roughly four in 10 churched adults qualify, saying they lead in some way at their church. The interpretation of "leader" here could be quite broad, including staff, deacons, elders, volunteer coordinators, team leaders or committee members; the survey did not limit leadership to senior or executive pastors. Barna researchers elected to cast a wide net for this grouping, with the goal of identifying those churchgoers who personally carry some sense of ownership and responsibility for the thriving of their church. Members of this group can provide holistic and honest opinions as to how the church is being led and executing its vision.

As we look at the inner workings of ministries, we find some organizational gaps, as well as wisdom to help pastors and leaders steward their time, energy and influence. ●

> Are Future-Focused

> Have Stable Resources

> Have Healthy Teams

> and Are Data-Informed

Future-Focused

Has your church set and communicated a vision for where it will be 10 years from now? Fifteen years from now? And how is your church strategically preparing for that future *today*?

A future-focused church is one with a clear, commonly understood vision for their future. Accordingly, this means being a church that believes the next generation is essential to the path forward. Three in five leaders (61%) confidently believe that their church is future-focused, reporting high scores (nine or 10) for both items.

Leaders who are relatively new to their church (those who say have been there two or fewer years) are far less likely to describe their church as future-focused (45%), suggesting that the Church today struggles to communicate and pass along vision to new leaders. Relatedly, young leaders are the least likely to give high marks for their church's communication of vision and empowerment of the next generation (49% of Gen Z, 53% Millennials, 72% Gen X, 60% Boomers). This may also stem from a healthy skepticism that Barna often hears voiced by young members of the Church today. In Barna's *Gen Z Vol. 2*, for instance, we see that only one-third of churched 13-to-21-year-olds agrees strongly that they have learned what it feels like to be part of a team at church (35%) or that they are given real chances to contribute to their church (32%).[48]

Numbers like these can help church leaders assess the potency of their vision as well as the presence of developmental gaps for future leaders. ●

Future-Focused

(scores 9 or 10 on individual items)
Base: identify as leaders in their church

Item 1: "There is a clear vision for the future of this church"	Item 2: "The next generation is essential to the future of this church"	Future-Focused (combined 1 & 2)
65%	66%	61%

n=410 U.S. churched adults, September 16–October 4, 2021.

Resource Stability

This aspect of thriving churches is perhaps obvious: Effective ministry takes time, money and people.

It may also *seem* obvious that bigger, wealthier churches would be more likely to thrive—but there are nuanced ways to understand how churches approach stewardship. Barna's research suggests measuring the stability, not necessarily the amount, of fiscal and personnel resources within an organization—in other words, quality rather than quantity. Fifty-six percent of leaders offer high scores for the resource stability of their church, meaning they have financial optimism and believe their church has enough volunteers and leaders to operate effectively.

Financial well-being, organizationally and personally, can be an especially frustrating area for church leaders today. In Barna's *The State of Pastors*, "financial and administrative duties" was found to be the third worst part of a pastor's job (19%), following "lack of commitment among laypeople" (35%) and "low spiritual maturity" (27%).[49] Furthermore, *The State of Pastors* explored the effects of a pastor's personal financial flourishing on the health of a church body. Analysts found that financial uncertainty is closely related to discontent with the ministry; pastors who see themselves as struggling or merely stable financially (as opposed to secure) express lower levels of satisfaction with their vocation or with their current position.[50]

These are fraught topics—but many churchgoers are eager to hear about them. Consider that money is the number-one thing Black Church churchgoers wish their churches would approach differently.[51]

These data points illustrate how important resource stability is for the thriving of a church, the well-being and health of leaders and the confidence of congregants. ●

Resource Stability
(scores 9 or 10 on individual items)
Base: identify as leaders in their church

| Item 1: "I am optimistic about the financial stability of this church going forward" | Item 2: "This church has enough leaders and volunteers to operate effectively" | Resource Stability (combined 1 & 2) |

n=410 U.S. churched adults, September 16–October 4, 2021.

Team Health

In the fall of 2020, Barna analysts uncovered something concerning: Only half of pastors (51%) agree strongly that the members of their leadership team trust each other. Agreement was even weaker among leaders under the age of 50 (42%) and among ethnic minorities (31%).[52] This emphasized a trend Barna has been observing for years: Team health and well-being appear fragile in many churches today.

In Barna's assessment, team health is measured by two items that are especially telling of the nature of a church's leadership dynamic: role clarity and internal trust among the leadership. With these combined items, three in five leaders (62%) report high levels of team health in their church. Millennial leaders are the least likely to offer high scores (54%).

Team health may be something that grows with time. Leaders who have been at their church for two or fewer years are less likely to say they have team health (50% vs. 69% of those who have been at their church for 3–10 years, 71% for 11+ years).

Pursuing peace and guarding against strife are spiritual skills with personal and organizational benefits for leaders. In *The State of Pastors*, Barna researchers found a strong correlation between high risk of burnout for a pastor and relational challenges within the church's leadership.[53] The data indicate a strong, mutually supportive relationship between a pastor and his or her team is integral to church health and to the pastor's health. Relational harmony and role clarity may lower the risk of burning out, lengthen team tenure and significantly boost church thriving. ●

Team Health

(scores 9 or 10 on individual items)
Base: identify as leaders in their church

Item 1: "I am clear about the expectations of my role"	Item 2: "The trust between church leaders internally is *excellent*"	Team Health (combined 1 & 2)
63%	66%	62%

n=410 U.S. churched adults, September 16–October 4, 2021.

Data-Informed

What does it mean to be a data-informed church? To put it in simple terms, a data-informed church is one that has the data needed to make well-informed ministry decisions and has good systems in place to know and track attendees.

Barna research suggests that, for about half of churches today, data-informed leadership is lacking. Fifty-four percent of churched adults who call themselves leaders give their church a high score for this dimension, making it the lowest performing dimension in the leading-related categories of thriving churches. This gap is especially apparent among non-mainline churches, which might lack some of the instruments that older or more established denominations provide (48% vs. 64% of mainline and 60% of Catholic leaders report high scores).

Building data-informed leaders is one of Barna's primary goals, so let's dig deeper into the role that data already plays in the Church today.

Four in 10 churched adults (41%) tell Barna that they know their church is tracking engagement and attendance behaviors. One in three (34%) says their church does not do this, but one in four (24%) admits they don't know if this is the case. A notable 33 percent of Boomers and 40 percent of Elders report that they don't know, revealing a generational divide surrounding clarity on the role that data might play in church life today. According to leaders (who arguably have more visibility into their church's systems), two-thirds (67%) say their church is in fact monitoring engagement.

For those congregants who know their engagement is being tracked, the majority reports that this data is infused into church communications. In the past six months, 71 percent say they have heard attendance

Data-Informed

(scores 9 or 10 on individual items)
Base: identify as leaders in their church

Item 1: "As a leader, I have the data I need to make well-informed ministry decisions"

Item 2: "We have good systems in place to know and track our people"

Data-Informed (combined 1 & 2)

n=410 U.S. churched adults, September 16–October 4, 2021.

What Are Some Common Traits of Churched Adults Who Lead?

Most churched adults who identify as leaders in some capacity (not just executive or senior pastors) are married and have children in their home. They tend to be Millennials (41%), but notable proportions of other generations are involved with their churches to this degree (11% are Gen Z, 31% Gen X, 14% Boomers, 3% Elders). Churched adults who take on leadership functions lean toward being more educated; 52 percent have college degrees (27% have a high school or less education, 21% have completed some college or vocational training). Interestingly, leaders are no more likely to attend church services consistently (weekly), or to report signs of a flourishing faith, even though they are more likely to be involved with church programs, groups or ministries beyond the main service (69% participate weekly vs. 27% of non-leaders).

data talked about in a sermon, and 62 percent know it has been a driver for church strategy.

With good reason, some pastors wrestle with how to lead in a data-informed way while also respecting congregational comfort and security. For the most part, churched adults seem to have faith their churches will shoulder that responsibility well. Eighty-nine percent agree they are willing to give personal information to their church (58% strongly, 31% somewhat). Churched adults tend to say knowing their church is tracking their engagement makes them feel safe, like they're part of something, trusting of the leaders they're following and cared for. On the other hand, very few voice concern or say they feel nervous, violated or uncomfortable about their church tracking their engagement. Even among churched adults whose engagement is *not* tracked by their churches, there is more uncertainty than outright pushback to the idea of churches monitoring attendees. Among young congregants in particular, it may even bolster feelings of trust and safety.

However, some churched adults share discomfort with sharing their information, especially when they are not committed to a church. Visitors especially would feel uncomfortable if their information or activity were tracked. Likewise, many newcomers are cautious with their

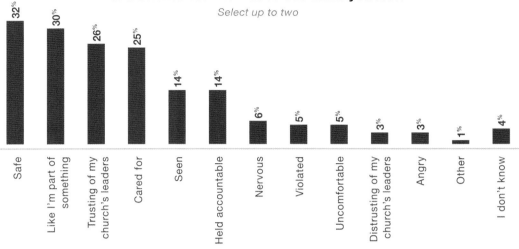

You have said that your church tracks your engagement and attendance. How does this make you feel?

Select up to two

- Safe — 32%
- Like I'm part of something — 30%
- Trusting of my church's leaders — 26%
- Cared for — 25%
- Seen — 14%
- Held accountable — 14%
- Nervous — 6%
- Violated — 5%
- Uncomfortable — 5%
- Distrusting of my church's leaders — 3%
- Angry — 3%
- Other — 1%
- I don't know — 4%

n=407 U.S. churched adults who say their church is tracking their engagement and attendance behaviors, September 18–October 4, 2021.

personal data. Almost one in five churched adults (17%) says they wouldn't be open to sharing any of their personal information, not even their name, when visiting a new church. This is especially true of older generations (13% of Gen Z, 14% Millennials, 11% Gen X, 23% Boomers, 27% Elders). When it comes to data-informed leadership, churches must balance concern for the comfort of newcomers while strategically building a culture of belonging for faithful attendees.

Many congregants are open to sharing information when they're committed to a church and, even more so, they believe their church might be better for it. That's true just for *basic* measures of engagement—outside these measures, there is potential to gain more nuanced impressions of the flourishing of a congregation and the thriving of a church. In picking up this book, you are likely already curious about what it means to measure what matters. What might it look like to grow in your capacity as a data-informed leader? ●

METRICS FOR STAYING ON MISSION

A Q&A WITH ED STETZER

Author, missiologist and executive director of the Billy Graham Center at Wheaton College

Q: What can church leaders be measuring today? What should they pay attention to?

A: Most pastors know what their attendance is and what their giving is. But we need to change the scorecard in church. We need to expand it to include what it means to be a disciple, a follower of Jesus on mission in the broken and hurting world we live in. Patterns of congregational life have shifted. Some have become more involved, giving more, serving more. [However], many of the loosely involved or nominally connected have completely disconnected. We must learn to keep measuring but measure differently [and have] a mission-driven approach to our metrics.

Q: Has the pandemic redefined "church?"

A: There are marks of a church that need to be true in every time and every place. But we have recreated church in the modern image. We've got to help people think of church not as a place but as a people. For too many of us, church is a service, at a time, with a certain expected product, and that's produced a consumer-driven [mentality]. Now we have a bunch of customers. What we really need are co-laborers. Some people stepped up, stood out and filled in the gap [during the disruption of the pandemic]. What we need to do now is help the rest of the congregation move into that co-laboring space, and then, ultimately, labor together.

Q: Why is it important for churches to engage the mission right now?

A: We've learned most Christians are [growing spiritually] on their own, and their church is a thing on the side. We need to bring church and the covenant community that it is back into greater focus. Then, engage the mission. The moment we're in doesn't pause the mission we're on. Jesus came to save the lost, and he served the hurting. We need a renewed focus on churches having fresh, new energy elevating their ecclesiology. Then, engage the mission to show and share the love of Jesus in their context around the world. ●

What's keeping people from returning to church? Ed Stetzer explains.

MORE THAN NUMBERS

A Q&A WITH NANCY DUARTE

Communication expert, author and CEO of Duarte

Q: Do you have advice for church leaders about navigating the data they use to communicate or make decisions? What are some dos and don'ts, especially for those who aren't so data-savvy?

A: Whether in ministry or in life, you can't manipulate. You can't twist the statistics. You should never state a statistic in isolation without explaining the context of it or the source of it.

People approach a data set and say, "Oh, I want to find data that supports my already strongly held belief." I say, go in and pursue data from places that come to the *opposite* conclusion and consider them too. If you don't consider that there is an alternate truth out there, you won't be able to persuade your audience. Even if you are pursuing the data to confirm what you already believe, you have to consider data that say otherwise and mention it. If you don't, you're going to come off as entrenched or approaching everything with bias. For church leaders and pastors, some people won't be open to your message if you're referring to a biased go-to source only.

Q: Traditional metrics for church health have been changing, especially through the pandemic. What would you share with church leaders and pastors who are figuring out how to measure what matters most in their context?

A: There is a fine line in how the Church uses data, because the most valuable data is immeasurable. It's love. It's the currency of heaven, and it's absolutely immeasurable. How do you measure that somebody's heart has transformed? How do you measure a heart that forgives? When they walked in the room, what was their way of behaving and believing? How do you know? After they heard the message and left the room, what was their new way of behaving and believing? It's so hard to measure, but that is measuring the heart of man. It is different than measuring the quantity of people who came through the door.

In my own organization, we're not always about the numbers. Humans are bigger than that. Humans are better than that. Culture is not the numbers. I want to make sure that we value as many immeasurables as measurables. It is not lost on us that what makes our organization effervescent, you can't measure in a number, ever. ●

LEADING WELL AND LEARNING TO ADAPT

A Q&A WITH BISHOP CLAUDE ALEXANDER

Senior pastor of The Park Church in Charlotte, North Carolina

Q: How has shepherding people changed for you during the pandemic?

A: It has become more intentional. I hear Psalm 23 differently. When you read the words, "Makes me to lie down in green pastures, leads me beside still waters," there is a qualitative aspect of that. Not just pastures, *green* pastures. Not just waters, *still* waters. The shepherding task is as much concerned about the environment in which people are in as the quality, the safety and health of the environment.

Q: How have you challenged your congregants to deepen and share their faith in these times?

A: For some, challenge can be a strong motivator. The challenge from me, but also the challenge of the season motivated people to lean in. That combination helped create the environment for growth and deepening. Secondly, being able to reframe, to give a different way of looking at a challenge [was key]. Being able to say, "This is an opportunity" and allow people to see the presence of God in [difficult times]. There's a sense of God that we can get uniquely in this time.

[During the shutdown], we were no longer the church that gathered. But we can be the church that serves. We are most like Jesus when we give ourselves to redemptive service. We are most like the angels when we gather for worship. Perhaps, this is a time where God is seeking to shift us from the romance of the angelic to the romance of Jesus.

Q: You've been in ministry for decades. What shifts have you seen or anticipate for churches?

A: The shift from an individual-centered approach to a team. That's a big shift. When I was in seminary from, there was no training in terms of team ministry. It was all about you as an individual, you as a pastor. There's recognition today that the time is calling for a team, not just an individual. There's a return of the power for ministry to the laity and the essential nature of relationship for disciple making. The COVID-19 pandemic [nudged the Church] to move from individual congregational ministry to collaborative ministry between different churches. ●

The Park Church saw unique growth and engagement during the pandemic. Bishop Alexander explains how they did it.

TRUSTING DATA AND **BEING A** **TRUSTED LEADER**

A Q&A WITH RYAN BURGE

Author and assistant professor of political science at Eastern Illinois University

Q: What suggestions do you have for church leaders as they think about how research might show up in their sermons or staff discussions?

A: There's so much work being done in the sociology of religion that more pastors should be aware of. Pastors are trained to think theologically about the world and with a vertical orientation as their primary mode of understanding the world around them. But the Church has a horizontal dimension as well. We need to be more mindful of how human beings relate to each other. Sociology, psychology, political science and economics all speak to that horizontal dimension.

Use Google Scholar and other resources to search keywords and read articles and abstracts. Often, I'll use a study as a tent pole to craft my sermon around. This can be powerful. An interesting fact will stick in their head.

Q: What can church leaders and pastors do to be trusted as sources for their congregations and communities?

A: We're seeing a fundamental shift in authority in this country. Pastors must prove to their congregations that they deserve a megaphone. They have to become a trusted translator for what's going on in the world, and you cannot do that overnight. You do this by being transparent; by saying, "I don't know everything," "I'm unsure," "I'm changing my mind." If I'm humble, open and transparent, I'm going to expect [and see] my congregation to be open, humble and transparent.

Q: What encouraging data are you seeing within the Church today?

A: Churches are good social safety nets. We are very good at providing support for people, especially when they need it in their worst moment. If you get sick, they'll bring casserole dishes. If you need a job, someone to watch your kids, these social safety net situations that are hard to measure quantitatively [but important].

Looking at data, you also see people who are still going to church and engaged are just as religious today as they were 30 or 40 years ago. One of the myths is that America is a lot less religious today. But if you take out the "nones" (those who don't identify with a specific religious affiliation), America is just as religious today as it was 30 years ago. In addition, the share of people who attend church weekly is higher now. There's also strong data from multiple sources that say churches financially did well during COVID. ●

CARING FOR THE
FUTURE CHURCH

A Q&A WITH REV. DR. BRIANNA K. PARKER

Researcher and founder of Black Millennial Cafe

Q: What do you see in the data that indicates or reaffirms for you the fact that Black Church is alive and well?

A: When we looked at Gen Z and saw that they were still hopeful, that was really important for us. Especially concerning things like leadership of the church and how important it was for them to know that the leadership and staff at the church really cared about the congregation. It pretty much signaled that they were saying, "Come see about me. It's important that the leadership cares about what I'm doing." This shouldn't be unexpected, because the best programming in any church, definitely in the Black Church, happens in children's and youth ministry. Gen Z are going to believe that the leadership matters, maybe in ways that older young adults, or Boomers or Gen X won't be able to see. Programming kind of wanes after a while, and the relationship with leadership changes. That was extremely important for us to see and mark.

Q: What are some key issues that will affect Black churches' ability to continue to thrive in the future?

A: Forty-one percent of Black adults want church services to stay hybrid. When people are deciding to stay hybrid, it's not against you; that's their way to stay *with* you. Don't fight them on this! If you need to have a separate guide or curriculum for people who want to be hybrid, do that and allow that to follow your ministry so they can stay close.

People want to know that when they click [to join your online service], you're going to be worth their time. I'm *not* saying to get smoke and lights; I *am* saying to make sure you have content that is worth people watching. People are saying they want to stay hybrid—they're not saying they want to leave! Don't forget that. Stop giving up things that nobody wants you to take away. I think we should be encouraged by what's happening digitally.

Figure out how to own your digital space, whether that is through SEO, whether that is through email for communication.

I clearly still believe in the Black Church. We have every reason to believe in the Black Church. We have lost some footing, indeed, but we have some really manageable fixes to get us where we want to be, because we are still valuable in this world and definitely in this country. ●

Parker was a lead researcher and partner in Barna's Trends in the Black Church *project. This Q&A is adapted from her comments during a panel discussing the release of the research.*

USING RESEARCH STRATEGICALLY

A Q&A WITH MARK CHAVES

Professor of sociology, professor of religious studies and divinity at Duke University and director of the National Congregations Study

Q: How have you seen data impact church decisions?

A: Many feel, "We're not doing well as a church," or "We're not doing enough for the community," or "We're not doing enough to serve our people and our neighborhoods." The National Congregations Study has sometimes helped people recognize that, compared to churches in general, they're doing OK, or they're doing a lot of community engagement, or that they're actually above average in some respects. In this way, data that allow you to see how you fit into a bigger picture can be a morale booster, particularly when it comes to community engagement.

On the negative side, people can mistake correlation for causation. They say, "Churches with a certain worship style seem to be successful, so that must be *why* they're successful. If we emulate that, we'll be successful." That's an example of mistaking correlation for causation, when leaders do things because they think the research shows it will lead to certain types of desirable outcomes, when really the research only shows that certain characteristics tend to occur together.

More generally, there's a lot of misinterpretation and misunderstanding of research results out there. An important challenge for leaders is not just being up on the latest survey results, but being able to distinguish between solid and less-than-solid research results, between what's supported by a variety of evidence from a variety of sources (and, so, more likely to be true) compared to a one-off result from a single source, which should be received with more skepticism. Part of being truly data-informed is being able to discern that sort of difference between different kinds of research results.

Q: What societal trends are you paying attention to right now?

A: Religiosity, meaning individuals' religious belief and practice, has been declining slowly for decades, something that wasn't clear until relatively recently. We need to continue to track these trends, especially the generational differences in religiosity that are a big part of producing those trends.

I also track trends that aren't about growth or decline, but just changes in congregations. An important one we've been tracking is changes in worship in the direction of more informal and contemporary styles. Another important trend is increasing ethnic diversity in congregations. And then there's the aging of the churchgoing population and of the clergy. Fewer people are choosing to go into ministry as a career right out of college, and we see the effects of that in the aging of the clergy population. There also continues to be increased political and ideological polarization that's affecting churches and that's important to continue to track. ●

A Field Guide for
Thriving Digital Ministry

What a 90-Year-Old Episcopal Church Learned Through the Pandemic

Three tips shared through the stories of Reverend Drew Van Culin, rector of Christ Church in Grosse Pointe, Michigan

1. **Give more than scraps to virtual worship.** "In our case, it meant the installation of the camera system and video system that really captures our worship effectively. We anticipated that virtual worship would be with us for the future, so we made a meaningful investment, both in terms of the infrastructure but also the process of worship planning for a hybrid environment."

2. **Social media does not equal community.** "We've been aware of social media and utilizing social media for nearly 20 years now as a society. But we really saw how ineffective social media was for generating real connection and community. It tells you what's going on, but it's not the same."

3. **Keep the "old-school" methods that work.** "What a difference a phone call is compared to a Zoom meeting when you're trying to connect with somebody personally! We've leaned into those aspects of real-life, person-to-person community, and that's been really rewarding."

Podcast-Friendly Preaching

On the other side of the screen, congregants may struggle to focus on sermons-as-usual in a digital context.

John E. Perez, pastor of Faith Temple Church of God in Christ (Beacon, New York) shares how he's been stretched as a teacher and learned to recognize opportunities to better connect with his congregation.

"I had to learn to really change the way I deliver," Perez says. "People don't want to hear you for 90 minutes! I had to cut down my messages. I heard this quote by Tony Morgan, and I really appreciated it—he mentioned our service has got to be more like a podcast. They've got to be short, sweet and concise. So, I had to take out all the 'church-ese,' all that stuff, and really speak to the very heart of the community that I serve."

DATA IN ACTION:
PICK A NEW BENCHMARK

Measuring what matters isn't just about having the right metrics; it's also about picking the right standards to measure against. This is especially important in seasons like the years surrounding the pandemic.

Carey Nieuwhof, leadership expert and co-host of Barna's *ChurchPulse Weekly* podcast, recommends resetting benchmarks to manage expectations. "The world that existed in 2019 is dead, and to try to get back to where you were is a mistake," he wrote on his blog. "People resigned, moved, bailed, changed habits and disappeared. It's a new world now. Please don't delete your historical data (including your 2019 data), but don't get stuck on it either. Instead, perhaps pick 2021 as your new starting point. Or as time goes on, 2022. Set that as the benchmark because that year reflects the new era and reality."

Make Online Connections to Help Your Church Thrive

- What staff or volunteer positions might be created for different skillsets within your church to support hybrid ministry and re-source stability (technological experts, elder support, chat facilitators, etc.)?
- How can your digital worship promote Bible-centeredness? How can you place greater knowledge of scripture just a click away for online attendees?
- Instead of focusing on what's missing in online worship, how can you make use of tools and analytics that you wouldn't usually have in an in-person service to become more data-informed?
- How can online tools strengthen the clarity of communication from your leadership and nurture trust in churchgoers?
- Does the next generation's familiarity and ease with technology change how you think about leadership development for a hybrid church future?

Staying on Mission (and Going on Prayer Walks) Online

Some qualities of thriving churches, like social impact or prayer culture, might take new forms in a digital environment. Toni Mihal of Church on the Ridge (Snoqualmie, Washington) shares how her church hosted a virtual prayer experience for their congregation, focused on supporting their missions program. These meetings included talking about the importance of prayer, hearing from missionary partners—and even a virtual prayer walk.

"We had our partner in Latvia film an actual walk around the district where they ministered to the women on the streets. As a church, we were able to pray over that area without being there, and at the same time, our people were able to experience a prayer walk, which otherwise they would have never done."

Don't Lose Sight of the Online Attendee

One expert consulted for this report shared about finding a church that excelled at digital ministry when the pandemic surged. "A super clean set, eye contact, beautifully crafted words … I felt so *there*," she says. "That was when I decided, 'Wow, I'm going to make this my church home.'"

The problem: This church was in another state. When in-person services resumed, the pastor's eye contact with the camera was gone. She began to feel like a "voyeurist" in the worship experience.

She contacted the ministry and asked how to build community with others attending remotely. "How we continue to show up as we go in a blended environment is either going to isolate people or make them feel more connected," she says."

Even if your top priority is the local, physical congregation, how can you be intentional about helping members of your virtual congregation connect to God and to others? How can an excellent streamed service be augmented in a way that leads to greater discipleship and community offscreen as well? And do you make a point to really *see* your virtual congregants in services?

A Field Guide for
Teaching & Leading with Data

Numbers Don't Have to Bore Your Audience

Even if you aren't a statistician or a data nerd, you can incorporate research as you teach, disciple and connect with your team or congregants. Here are a few pointers for sharing data points confidently and creatively.

- Lean on charts or visual aids via handouts or onscreen.
- Assume most people don't know what to do with percentages alone. Break down statistics with fractions (as in, "two out of five Christians"). You might want to contextualize percentages by pointing out or engaging that same proportion of people in the room.
- Your congregation can help you understand and humanize the data too—especially if it represents them. For instance, in your efforts to reach the next generation, maybe you could sit down with young adults and get their candid insights on the data that reflects people of their age.
- If you're collecting congregational surveys, be open and transparent about the intent and the process. Share results honestly and in a timely manner, addressing the outcomes with sincerity and taking next steps seriously.

Does Data "Go Bad?"

Survey data can become dated, depending on how cultural shifts and stages of life may affect respondents, their context or the topic at hand. In a sense, data doesn't truly expire; it may always have something to teach you, as long as it is interpreted as it was collected: to learn about a specific group, in a specific time, in a specific place. If you're planning to communicate about a study or statistic, make it a practice to check if there is more recent data from that same source or other respected researchers; you may want to either update your information or look for changes over time.

In addition, as you collect data for your own ministry through the ChurchPulse or other assessments, consider the appropriate cadence for repeating surveys in order to keep an updated snapshot and track the health of your leadership and congregation.

DATA IN ACTION:
AN "A-HA MOMENT"

In recent years, many pastors have expressed surprise at Barna's finding that half of practicing Christians have heard of the Great Commission. "I was floored," says Toni Mihal, director of adult ministries, missions and outreach for Church on the Ridge (Snoqualmie, Washington). She first encountered this stat in Barna's *Activating Missions* CoLab, a learning cohort—and it was galvanizing. "That's when I realized that if I wanted to move my church forward in missions, I needed to understand where my church was in relation to knowing the Great Commission, but also our plan for missions as a whole. ... I was able to survey our congregation and find out where they are in the spectrum of so many things, not just their knowledge of the Great Commission."

10 Discussion Questions to Help Teams Engage Responsibly with Research

1. Do we trust this source?
2. Are there other reports, experts or books to help us learn more about the subject?
3. What finding is most surprising?
4. Were any of our assumptions or hunches validated?
5. Were any of our blind spots revealed?
6. Does any of the data confuse us or raise more questions?
7. What does this mean for how we can better support and shepherd our congregation?
8. What does this reveal about people we aren't yet reaching?
9. In light of this research, what do we need to start doing?
10. In light of this research, what do we need to stop doing?

DATA IN ACTION:
ASKING BETTER QUESTIONS

Pure Heart Church (Glendale, Arizona) includes two physical campuses, one of which is the result of a recent merger, and a virtual campus. Altogether, demographics and needs are shifting across the congregation. Brian Carson, pastor of pastoral care, says, "Data has been most helpful over the past five years to help staff ask better questions." For example, data helped them identify needs through the pandemic and as they "moved the dial" with a new focus on schools, reaching students, teachers, administrators and parents.

Brian also describes a turning point where he was reacquainted with the concept of predictive analytics. "We could empower church leaders to not only teach and address felt needs and biblical truths, but intentionally help people to make real change."

Consider the Internal & External Uses of Data

One expert encourages thinking about your own church ecosystem as you use data to make decisions or communicate. Data could be used externally in service of your oration or your sermon. Data could be used internally in service of managing your church, perhaps by monitoring activities, identifying needs and communicating with your staff about internal metrics. Data could also be used in service of leading your church, perhaps by casting vision and wrestling with the big picture or national norms. When you encounter an encouraging, challenging or thought-provoking piece of information, consider how it might show up in or impact each sphere of decision-making and communication.

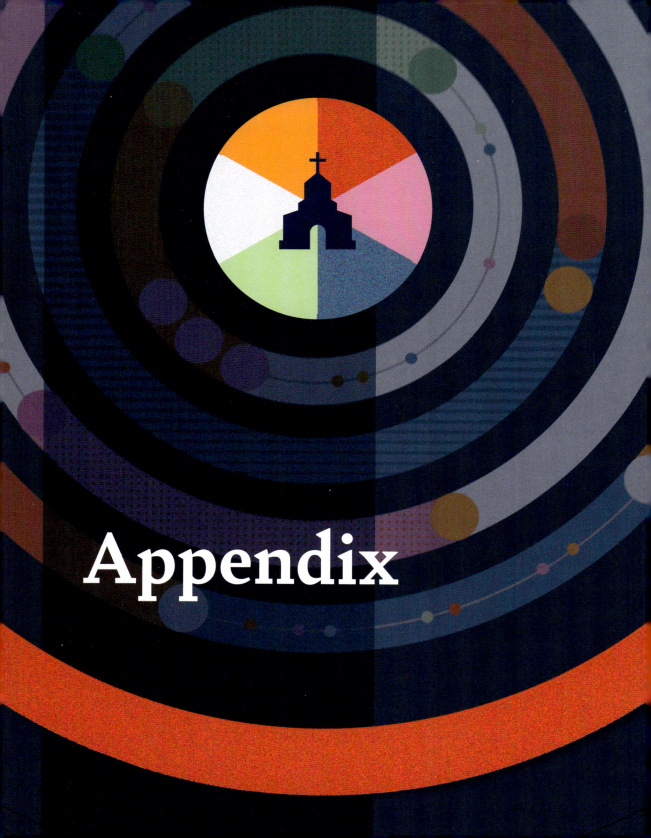

Appendix

Taking the Pulse of the Church

Here's a closer, more technical look at how Barna approached its research on flourishing people and thriving churches, as well as how the ChurchPulse assessment was developed.

How We Studied Flourishing People

When it came to studying human flourishing, Barna had a substantial research foundation to build upon. Alongside analysts at Gloo, the researchers started with validated studies on human flourishing and growing faith from Harvard, REVEAL, the Christian Life Profile and Barna's own research going back nearly four decades. The study was focused on five categories or "dimensions:" relationships, vocation, finances, well-being and faith.

In an initial nationally representative survey, U.S. adults (including those who regularly attended church) were asked about more than 50 items related to human flourishing. Using statistical tools such as factor analysis, data scientists then determined two items per dimension that most correlate with positive outcomes such as contentment, joy and hope among churchgoers and U.S. adults. Narrowing these items aided in creating a shorter, focused assessment for the ChurchPulse.

Barna has and will continue to gather national data using this final set of 10 questions to track trends related to human flourishing in the Church. Additionally, churches can deploy the ChurchPulse assessment and get a local, congregational view of how their own people are flourishing.

How We Studied Thriving Churches

Barna analysts worked with leaders across a spectrum of churches, as well as church consultants and researchers, to distill a list of possible qualities of thriving churches.

Based on this broad input, a beta survey of 31 U.S. congregations of varying sizes, regions, denominations and demographics looked at how well churches are accomplishing their objectives. Initially, there were 120 questions. Some of these apply to all churchgoers, some apply to those with a level of leadership investment in a congregation.

Using statistical tools and predictive modeling methods, analysts sought to explore organizational thriving beyond numeric growth or financial stability. Specifically, Barna looked at the relationship between the list of dimensions and qualities like: human flourishing, life satisfaction, congregants' intent to stay at their current church, congregants' "net promoter score" of their current church and self-reported spiritual growth.

Following this analysis, Barna conducted a nationally representative survey of churched adults, including some who identified as leaders, to establish norms for the final set of 30 questions. Barna will continue to gather national data to track trends related to thriving churches. Additionally, churches can deploy the ChurchPulse assessment and get a local, congregational view of how their own organizational thriving.

Skip the guesswork. Get custom insights on the flourishing and thriving of your congregation through the ChurchPulse.

Faith
Flourishing People

In Barna's research of human flourishing, the "faith" dimension is a high-level rating of spiritual vitality among Christians. *These questions were only asked of self-identified Christians.*

Churched Adults' Views of Jesus in Their Life

"I desire Jesus to be first in my life."

● 0 Disagree strongly ● 1 ● 2 ● 3 ● 4 ● 5 ● 6 ● 7 ● 8 ● 9 ● 10 Agree strongly

	0	1	2	3	4	5	6	7	8	9	10
All self-identified Christians	5%	2%	1%	3%	2%	14%	7%	9%	9%	10%	39%
Churched adults	1%	0%	0%	1%	1%	4%	5%	9%	13%	12%	55%
Practicing Christians	0%	0%	0%	0%	0%	1%	1%	5%	10%	12%	72%
Leaders	1%	0%	0%	1%	1%	3%	4%	10%	14%	14%	53%
Non-leaders	1%	0%	1%	0%	1%	4%	5%	8%	12%	10%	56%
Married churched adults	1%	0%	0%	1%	1%	2%	4%	9%	12%	14%	55%
Single churched adults	1%	0%	1%	0%	1%	6%	5%	9%	13%	10%	53%
Churched adults who have children under 18 in their household	1%	0%	1%	1%	1%	2%	5%	10%	13%	14%	52%
Churched adults who do not have children under 18 in the household	1%	0%	0%	1%	1%	5%	4%	8%	13%	11%	56%

U.S. Churched Adults' Faith Flourishing Score

85
Out of 100

Levels of Faith Flourishing

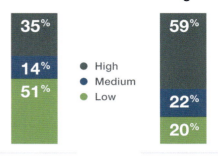

- ● High
- ● Medium
- ● Low

All Christians   Churched adults

Churched Adults' Views on the Bible's Authority in Their Life

"I believe the Bible has authority over what I say and do."

● 0 Disagree strongly   ● 1   ● 2   ● 3   ● 4   ● 5   ● 6   ● 7   ● 8   ● 9   ● 10 Agree strongly

	0	1	2	3	4	5	6	7	8	9	10
All self-identified Christians	9%	3%	4%	3%	4%	16%	9%	8%	8%	9%	26%
Churched adults	2%	1%	1%	1%	1%	6%	5%	9%	15%	17%	42%
Practicing Christians	1%	0%	0%	0%	0%	2%	2%	6%	14%	19%	54%
Leaders	1%	0%	0%	0%	1%	5%	3%	10%	15%	22%	42%
Non-leaders	3%	1%	1%	1%	2%	7%	7%	9%	14%	12%	42%
Married churched adults	1%	0%	0%	1%	1%	5%	5%	9%	15%	18%	44%
Single churched adults	3%	1%	1%	1%	2%	7%	5%	10%	15%	15%	40%
Churched adults who have children under 18 in their household	2%	0%	0%	0%	2%	4%	6%	8%	15%	22%	41%
Churched adults who do not have children under 18 in the household	2%	1%	1%	1%	1%	7%	5%	10%	15%	14%	43%

n=722 U.S. self-identified Christian adults, April 28–May 5, 2020;
n=1,003 U.S. churched adults, September 16–October 4, 2021.

Relationships
Flourishing People

In Barna's research of human flourishing, the "relationships" dimension looks at levels of satisfaction and contentment in close relationships.

Churched Adults' Level of Contentment with Their Relationships

"I am content with my friendships and relationships."

● 0 Disagree strongly　● 1　● 2　● 3　● 4　● 5　● 6　● 7　● 8　● 9　● 10　Agree strongly

	0	1	2	3	4	5	6	7	8	9	10
All U.S. adults	2%	1%	2%	3%	3%	16%	8%	14%	16%	12%	22%
Churched adults	1%	0%	1%	1%	2%	4%	5%	9%	17%	18%	40%
Practicing Christians	1%	0%	0%	2%	2%	4%	4%	7%	14%	18%	49%
Leaders	1%	1%	1%	1%	1%	3%	3%	9%	13%	19%	48%
Non-leaders	2%	0%	1%	2%	4%	6%	6%	10%	19%	18%	34%
Married churched adults	0%	1%	0%	1%	1%	3%	3%	8%	17%	20%	46%
Single churched adults	2%	0%	2%	2%	4%	7%	7%	11%	17%	17%	32%
Churched adults with children under 18 in their household	1%	1%	1%	0%	2%	3%	3%	9%	16%	16%	48%
Churched adults without children under 18 in their household	1%	0%	1%	2%	3%	5%	5%	10%	17%	20%	35%

U.S. Churched Adults' Relational Flourishing Score

82

Out of 100

Levels of Relational Flourishing

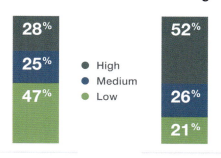

	High	Medium	Low

All U.S. adults: 28% High, 25% Medium, 47% Low

Churched adults: 52% High, 26% Medium, 21% Low

Churched Adults' Level of Satisfaction with Their Relationships

"My relationships are as satisfying as I would want them to be."

● 0 Disagree strongly   ● 1   ● 2   ● 3   ● 4   ● 5   ● 6   ● 7   ● 8   ● 9   ● 10 Agree strongly

	0	1	2	3	4	5	6	7	8	9	10
All U.S. adults	3%	2%	4%	3%	5%	16%	8%	12%	17%	11%	18%
Churched adults	1%	1%	1%	2%	2%	5%	6%	11%	17%	23%	31%
Practicing Christians	1%	1%	1%	2%	2%	4%	5%	10%	15%	24%	36%
Leaders	0%	0%	1%	0%	1%	3%	4%	11%	17%	25%	37%
Non-leaders	2%	1%	2%	3%	2%	7%	7%	12%	18%	21%	26%
Married churched adults	1%	0%	0%	1%	2%	3%	5%	9%	16%	26%	37%
Single churched adults	2%	1%	2%	3%	2%	8%	6%	13%	18%	20%	24%
Churched adults with children under 18 in their household	1%	0%	1%	1%	2%	3%	6%	10%	16%	24%	37%
Churched adults without children under 18 in their household	2%	1%	1%	2%	1%	7%	6%	12%	18%	23%	27%

n=1,093 U.S. adults, November 11–29, 2019;
n=1,003 churched U.S. adults, September 16–October 4, 2021.

Vocation
Flourishing People

In Barna's research of human flourishing, the "vocation" dimension looks at the experience of purpose in one's daily activity.

Churched Adults on Whether Their Lives Feel Worthwhile

Overall, to what extent do you feel the things you do in your life are worthwhile?

● 0 Not at all worthwhile ● 1 ● 2 ● 3 ● 4 ● 5 ● 6 ● 7 ● 8 ● 9 ● 10 Completely worthwhile

All U.S. adults

| 2% | 1% | 2% | 2% | 4% | 14% | 8% | 13% | 19% | 14% | 21% |

Churched adults

| 1% | 0% | 1% | 1% | 2% | 7% | 7% | 11% | 22% | 20% | 29% |

Practicing Christians

| 1% | 0% | 1% | 1% | 1% | 5% | 5% | 10% | 20% | 22% | 35% |

Leaders

| 0% | 0% | 0% | 1% | 2% | 4% | 6% | 10% | 20% | 22% | 35% |

Non-leaders

| 1% | 1% | 1% | 2% | 2% | 9% | 8% | 12% | 23% | 18% | 25% |

Married churched adults

| 0% | 0% | 0% | 1% | 2% | 4% | 5% | 11% | 22% | 21% | 34% |

Single churched adults

| 1% | 1% | 1% | 2% | 2% | 9% | 9% | 12% | 21% | 18% | 24% |

Churched adults with children under 18 in their household

| 0% | 0% | 0% | 1% | 2% | 6% | 6% | 12% | 20% | 17% | 35% |

Churched adults without children under 18 in their household

| 1% | 1% | 1% | 2% | 2% | 7% | 7% | 11% | 22% | 21% | 26% |

U.S. Churched Adults' Vocational Flourishing Score

80
Out of 100

Levels of Vocational Flourishing

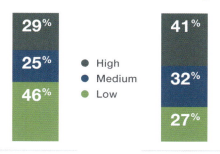

- High
- Medium
- Low

All U.S. adults
- 29%
- 25%
- 46%

Churched adults
- 41%
- 32%
- 27%

Churched Adults on Understanding Their Purpose

"I understand my purpose in life."

● 0 Disagree strongly ● 1 ● 2 ● 3 ● 4 ● 5 ● 6 ● 7 ● 8 ● 9 ● 10 Agree strongly

All U.S. adults

0	1	2	3	4	5	6	7	8	9	10
5%	2%	3%	3%	2%	17%	8%	11%	17%	12%	21%

Churched adults

| 1% | 1% | 1% | 2% | 2% | 7% | 7% | 13% | 19% | 16% | 31% |

Practicing Christians

| 2% | 0% | 1% | 1% | 1% | 6% | 6% | 9% | 20% | 17% | 37% |

Leaders

| 0% | 0% | 1% | 1% | 1% | 4% | 5% | 14% | 19% | 19% | 37% |

Non-leaders

| 2% | 2% | 2% | 2% | 2% | 9% | 10% | 12% | 19% | 14% | 26% |

Married churched adults

| 1% | 0% | 1% | 1% | 1% | 5% | 7% | 11% | 18% | 19% | 36% |

Single churched adults

| 2% | 2% | 2% | 3% | 2% | 9% | 8% | 16% | 21% | 12% | 24% |

Churched adults with children under 18 in their household

| 1% | 1% | 1% | 2% | 1% | 5% | 8% | 11% | 18% | 16% | 37% |

Churched adults without children under 18 in their household

| 2% | 1% | 2% | 1% | 2% | 8% | 7% | 14% | 20% | 16% | 27% |

n=1,093 U.S. adults, November 11–29, 2019;
n=1,003 U.S. churched adults, September 16–October 4, 2021.

Finances
Flourishing People

In Barna's research of human flourishing, the "finances" dimension measures the degree to which one worries about expenses and resources.

Churched Adults' Concern Around Monthly Living Expenses
How often do you worry about being able to meet normal monthly living expenses?

● 0 Worry all of the time ● 1 ● 2 ● 3 ● 4 ● 5 ● 6 ● 7 ● 8 ● 9 ● 10 Do not worry

	0	1	2	3	4	5	6	7	8	9	10
All U.S. adults	9%	2%	5%	6%	5%	17%	7%	11%	12%	9%	17%
Churched adults	6%	3%	4%	4%	4%	9%	8%	12%	16%	11%	22%
Practicing Christians	7%	3%	4%	5%	4%	8%	6%	10%	17%	12%	25%
Leaders	5%	2%	2%	3%	4%	9%	8%	14%	18%	13%	23%
Non-leaders	8%	3%	6%	5%	4%	10%	7%	10%	14%	10%	22%
Married churched adults	6%	4%	3%	5%	3%	7%	7%	12%	16%	13%	25%
Single churched adults	7%	2%	6%	4%	6%	12%	9%	11%	15%	9%	19%
Churched adults with children under 18 in their household	7%	4%	2%	4%	4%	8%	9%	12%	19%	11%	19%
Churched adults without children under 18 in their household	6%	3%	5%	5%	4%	10%	7%	11%	14%	11%	24%

U.S. Churched Adults' Financial Flourishing Score

68
Out of 100

Levels of Financial Flourishing

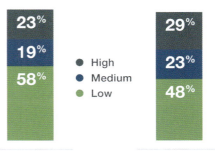

	High	Medium	Low
All U.S. adults	23%	19%	58%
Churched adults	29%	23%	48%

All U.S. adults

Churched adults

Churched Adults' Concern Around Life Necessities

How often do you worry about safety, food or housing?

● 0 Worry all of the time ● 1 ● 2 ● 3 ● 4 ● 5 ● 6 ● 7 ● 8 ● 9 ● 10 Do not worry

	0	1	2	3	4	5	6	7	8	9	10
All U.S. adults	5%	3%	3%	5%	6%	18%	8%	10%	12%	11%	19%
Churched adults	6%	2%	3%	4%	5%	9%	8%	13%	14%	12%	25%
Practicing Christians	5%	2%	3%	4%	5%	8%	6%	10%	15%	12%	30%
Leaders	5%	1%	3%	2%	4%	7%	9%	13%	16%	14%	25%
Non-leaders	6%	2%	4%	5%	6%	10%	8%	12%	13%	9%	24%
Married churched adults	5%	2%	3%	4%	4%	8%	7%	12%	16%	13%	27%
Single churched adults	6%	1%	4%	3%	6%	11%	10%	13%	13%	10%	22%
Churched adults with children under 18 in their household	7%	2%	3%	2%	4%	8%	10%	13%	17%	11%	22%
Churched adults without children under 18 in their household	5%	2%	4%	4%	5%	10%	8%	12%	13%	12%	26%

n=1,093 U.S. adults, November 11–29, 2019;
n=1,003 U.S. churched adults, September 16–October 4, 2021.

Well-Being
Flourishing People

In Barna's research of human flourishing, the "well-being" dimension looks at how one rates their physical and mental health.

Churched Adults' Assessment of Their Physical Health

In general, how would you rate your physical health?

● 0 Poor   ● 1   ● 2   ● 3   ● 4   ● 5   ● 6   ● 7   ● 8   ● 9   ● 10 Excellent

Group	0 Poor	1	2	3	4	5	6	7	8	9	10 Excellent
All U.S. adults	2%	1%	3%	5%	6%	15%	11%	15%	20%	10%	12%
Churched adults	1%	0%	1%	2%	3%	8%	8%	17%	24%	17%	19%
Practicing Christians	2%	0%	1%	2%	3%	8%	7%	17%	25%	17%	19%
Leaders	1%	0%	1%	1%	2%	6%	4%	13%	22%	19%	31%
Non-leaders	2%	1%	2%	3%	4%	9%	10%	19%	26%	15%	10%
Married churched adults	1%	0%	1%	2%	2%	5%	7%	15%	25%	19%	24%
Single churched adults	2%	0%	2%	2%	3%	11%	9%	19%	23%	14%	14%
Churched adults with children under 18 in their household	1%	0%	0%	1%	2%	4%	5%	14%	23%	19%	32%
Churched adults without children under 18 in their household	2%	1%	2%	3%	3%	10%	9%	19%	25%	15%	12%

U.S. Churched Adults' Well-Being Score

Levels of Well-Being

78 Out of 100

High
Medium
Low

All U.S. adults: 22% / 28% / 50%
Churched adults: 36% / 34% / 30%

Churched Adults' Assessment of Their Mental Health

In general, how would you rate your overall mental health?

● 0 Poor   ● 1   ● 2   ● 3   ● 4   ● 5   ● 6   ● 7   ● 8   ● 9   ● 10 Excellent

	0 Poor	1	2	3	4	5	6	7	8	9	10 Excellent
All U.S. adults	3%	2%	3%	4%	5%	13%	8%	10%	18%	15%	19%
Churched adults	1%	1%	1%	2%	3%	6%	6%	12%	19%	21%	30%
Practicing Christians	1%	1%	1%	1%	2%	4%	5%	11%	18%	23%	34%
Leaders	0%	0%	0%	1%	2%	5%	4%	11%	18%	23%	36%
Non-leaders	1%	1%	1%	3%	3%	7%	8%	13%	20%	20%	25%
Married churched adults	1%	0%	0%	1%	2%	4%	5%	9%	19%	25%	33%
Single churched adults	1%	1%	1%	3%	3%	9%	7%	15%	19%	16%	25%
Churched adults with children under 18 in their household	0%	0%	1%	1%	3%	4%	6%	12%	17%	23%	33%
Churched adults without children under 18 in their household	1%	1%	1%	2%	2%	7%	6%	12%	20%	21%	28%

n=722 U.S. self-identified Christian adults, April 28–May 5, 2020;
n=1,003 U.S. churched adults, September 16–October 4, 2021.

Worship Experience
Thriving Churches

In Barna's research of thriving churches, the "worship experience" dimension provides insight into how the main worship service is helping congregants feel more connected with God.

Churched Adults on Worship at Their Church

"I feel closer to God through the main worship service at this church."

● 0 Disagree strongly ● 1 ● 2 ● 3 ● 4 ● 5 ● 6 ● 7 ● 8 ● 9 ● 10 Agree strongly

	0	1	2	3	4	5	6	7	8	9	10
All churched adults	1%	1%	0%	1%	1%	5%	5%	11%	17%	18%	39%
Church tenure (2 or fewer years)	1%	1%	0%	1%	3%	7%	7%	13%	19%	19%	30%
Church tenure (3–10 years)	1%	1%	0%	2%	1%	4%	5%	12%	17%	19%	39%
Church tenure (10+ years)	1%	0%	0%	1%	0%	4%	3%	9%	16%	16%	49%
Weekly attendance	0%	0%	0%	1%	1%	4%	3%	11%	14%	19%	47%
Monthly attendance	1%	1%	0%	1%	1%	4%	8%	8%	20%	18%	38%
Less than monthly attendance	3%	1%	0%	1%	4%	7%	6%	18%	23%	15%	21%
Leaders	0%	0%	0%	1%	2%	3%	3%	9%	17%	21%	45%
Non-leaders	2%	1%	0%	1%	1%	7%	6%	13%	18%	16%	36%

U.S. Churched Adults' Worship Experience Score

83

Out of 100

Levels of Worship Experience

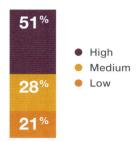

51%

28%

21%

● High
● Medium
● Low

Churched Adults on Experiencing God in Worship

How often do you leave this church's worship service feeling you have connected with God or personally experienced the presence of God?

● 0 Never ● 1 ● 2 ● 3 ● 4 ● 5 ● 6 ● 7 ● 8 ● 9 ● 10 Always

All churched adults

0 Never	1	2	3	4	5	6	7	8	9	10 Always
1%	0%	1%	1%	2%	6%	7%	11%	18%	19%	35%

Church tenure (2 or fewer years)

| 2% | 0% | 1% | 1% | 2% | 8% | 10% | 13% | 18% | 15% | 30% |

Church tenure (3–10 years)

| 1% | 0% | 1% | 1% | 2% | 7% | 7% | 10% | 19% | 22% | 32% |

Church tenure (10+ years)

| 0% | 0% | 1% | 0% | 1% | 4% | 3% | 10% | 18% | 19% | 42% |

Weekly attendance

| 1% | 0% | 0% | 0% | 1% | 5% | 5% | 9% | 16% | 21% | 41% |

Monthly attendance

| 1% | 0% | 0% | 1% | 1% | 6% | 8% | 11% | 20% | 19% | 32% |

Less than monthly attendance

| 2% | 1% | 3% | 2% | 3% | 8% | 10% | 15% | 20% | 13% | 23% |

Leaders

| 0% | 0% | 0% | 0% | 1% | 5% | 6% | 11% | 17% | 20% | 39% |

Non-leaders

| 2% | 0% | 1% | 1% | 2% | 8% | 7% | 11% | 19% | 17% | 32% |

n=1,003 U.S. churched adults, September 16–October 4, 2021.

Connected Community
Thriving Churches

In Barna's research of thriving churches, the "connected community" dimension looks at whether individuals are forming meaningful relationships, including in their churches.

Churched Adults' Perceptions of Connectedness Within Their Church

"This church provides a community where I feel connected."

● 0 Disagree strongly　● 1　● 2　● 3　● 4　● 5　● 6　● 7　● 8　● 9　● 10 Agree strongly

Group	0	1	2	3	4	5	6	7	8	9	10
All churched adults	1%	0%	1%	1%	2%	6%	6%	12%	18%	19%	35%
Church tenure (2 or fewer years)	1%	1%	1%	3%	2%	7%	7%	14%	19%	16%	29%
Church tenure (3–10 years)	1%	0%	1%	1%	1%	5%	6%	12%	18%	22%	33%
Church tenure (10+ years)	1%	1%	0%	1%	2%	5%	5%	10%	16%	19%	42%
Weekly attendance	0%	0%	0%	1%	1%	6%	5%	9%	17%	19%	42%
Monthly attendance	1%	1%	1%	2%	1%	5%	5%	14%	17%	22%	32%
Less than monthly attendance	2%	1%	1%	1%	4%	7%	9%	18%	19%	16%	21%
Leaders	0%	0%	0%	2%	1%	3%	3%	10%	18%	22%	40%
Non-leaders	1%	1%	1%	1%	3%	8%	7%	13%	17%	16%	31%

U.S. Churched Adults' Connected Community Score

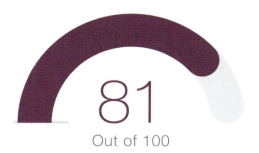

81
Out of 100

Levels of Connected Community

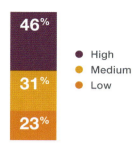

46% High
31% Medium
23% Low

Churched Adults' Perceptions of Relationships and Accountability

"This church helps me develop relationships that encourage accountability."

● 0 Disagree strongly ● 1 ● 2 ● 3 ● 4 ● 5 ● 6 ● 7 ● 8 ● 9 ● 10 Agree strongly

	0	1	2	3	4	5	6	7	8	9	10
All churched adults	1%	0%	1%	1%	2%	8%	6%	11%	22%	16%	31%
Church tenure (2 or fewer years)	2%	0%	1%	2%	4%	10%	5%	11%	21%	17%	27%
Church tenure (3–10 years)	1%	0%	1%	1%	2%	5%	8%	11%	23%	19%	30%
Church tenure (10+ years)	2%	0%	0%	2%	1%	10%	6%	9%	22%	13%	35%
Weekly attendance	1%	0%	0%	2%	2%	8%	5%	8%	23%	15%	36%
Monthly attendance	1%	0%	1%	1%	2%	7%	6%	12%	22%	19%	29%
Less than monthly attendance	2%	1%	2%	2%	4%	10%	11%	14%	20%	16%	20%
Leaders	0%	0%	0%	0%	2%	5%	4%	9%	22%	20%	37%
Non-leaders	2%	0%	1%	3%	2%	11%	8%	12%	22%	14%	26%

n=1,003 U.S. churched adults, September 16–October 4, 2021.

Prayer Culture
Thriving Churches

In Barna's research of thriving churches, the "prayer culture" looks at the habits and the power of prayer experiences in a church.

Churched Adults on Prayer Habits

"This church helps me develop habits of prayer that better connect me with God."

● 0 Disagree strongly ● 1 ● 2 ● 3 ● 4 ● 5 ● 6 ● 7 ● 8 ● 9 ● 10 Agree strongly

	0	1	2	3	4	5	6	7	8	9	10
All churched adults	1%	0%	0%	1%	1%	6%	6%	9%	18%	19%	38%
Church tenure (2 or fewer years)	2%	1%	0%	1%	1%	6%	7%	10%	21%	18%	32%
Church tenure (3–10 years)	0%	1%	1%	1%	1%	5%	4%	9%	20%	21%	37%
Church tenure (10+ years)	1%	0%	1%	1%	1%	5%	7%	8%	15%	17%	44%
Weekly attendance	0%	0%	0%	1%	1%	5%	5%	7%	16%	18%	46%
Monthly attendance	0%	1%	0%	0%	2%	5%	4%	9%	23%	20%	36%
Less than monthly attendance	3%	0%	1%	2%	2%	7%	11%	15%	19%	19%	20%
Leaders	0%	0%	0%	1%	2%	3%	3%	7%	18%	22%	44%
Non-leaders	1%	1%	1%	1%	1%	8%	8%	10%	19%	16%	34%

U.S. Churched Adults' Prayer Culture Score

84
Out of 100

Levels of Prayer Culture

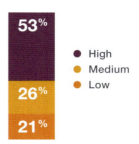

53%
26%
21%

- High
- Medium
- Low

Churched Adults on the Power of Prayer

"I have seen the power of prayer through this church."

● 0 Disagree strongly ● 1 ● 2 ● 3 ● 4 ● 5 ● 6 ● 7 ● 8 ● 9 ● 10 Agree strongly

	0	1	2	3	4	5	6	7	8	9	10
All churched adults	1%	1%	0%	1%	1%	5%	5%	8%	20%	17%	40%
Church tenure (2 or fewer years)	2%	1%	0%	1%	2%	7%	5%	10%	25%	16%	30%
Church tenure (3–10 years)	1%	0%	0%	2%	2%	5%	5%	7%	19%	20%	39%
Church tenure (10+ years)	0%	1%	0%	1%	0%	3%	6%	8%	15%	16%	49%
Weekly attendance	1%	0%	0%	1%	1%	4%	5%	7%	17%	18%	47%
Monthly attendance	0%	0%	1%	1%	1%	4%	5%	8%	21%	18%	40%
Less than monthly attendance	3%	2%	0%	2%	3%	8%	7%	13%	25%	15%	22%
Leaders	0%	0%	0%	1%	1%	4%	2%	6%	19%	22%	45%
Non-leaders	1%	1%	0%	2%	2%	6%	7%	10%	20%	14%	37%

n=1,003 U.S. churched adults, September 16–October 4, 2021.

Bible-Centeredness
Thriving Churches

In Barna's research of thriving churches, the "Bible-centeredness" dimension measures how well a church is helping congregants understand and live out biblical teachings.

Churched Adults on Basic Foundations of the Bible

How well does this church support your spiritual growth through helping you understand the basic foundations of the Bible?

● 0 Not well at all ● 1 ● 2 ● 3 ● 4 ● 5 ● 6 ● 7 ● 8 ● 9 ● 10 Very well

	0	1	2	3	4	5	6	7	8	9	10
All churched adults	1%	0%	0%	1%	1%	6%	6%	12%	17%	17%	37%
Church tenure (2 or fewer years)	2%	1%	0%	1%	2%	10%	7%	16%	15%	13%	33%
Church tenure (3–10 years)	1%	0%	1%	0%	2%	4%	8%	11%	18%	21%	35%
Church tenure (10+ years)	1%	0%	1%	1%	1%	5%	4%	11%	19%	15%	42%
Weekly attendance	1%	0%	0%	1%	1%	5%	4%	10%	17%	17%	44%
Monthly attendance	0%	1%	0%	0%	1%	4%	7%	14%	19%	19%	34%
Less than monthly attendance	3%	0%	1%	2%	2%	12%	12%	17%	16%	13%	21%
Leaders	0%	0%	0%	0%	2%	5%	4%	12%	16%	19%	42%
Non-leaders	1%	1%	1%	1%	1%	8%	8%	13%	19%	15%	33%

U.S. Churched Adults' Bible-Centeredness Score

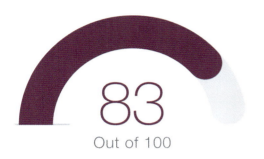

83
Out of 100

Levels of Bible-Centeredness

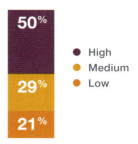

50%
29%
21%

● High
● Medium
● Low

Churched Adults on Living Out the Bible

"This church helps me live out the teachings of the Bible in my everyday life."

● 0 Not well at all   ● 1   ● 2   ● 3   ● 4   ● 5   ● 6   ● 7   ● 8   ● 9   ● 10   Very well

	0	1	2	3	4	5	6	7	8	9	10
All churched adults	1%	0%	1%	1%	1%	6%	5%	12%	18%	19%	36%
Church tenure (2 or fewer years)	2%	1%	1%	0%	1%	8%	5%	14%	17%	16%	34%
Church tenure (3–10 years)	0%	0%	1%	1%	1%	5%	5%	10%	19%	24%	34%
Church tenure (10+ years)	1%	0%	0%	1%	1%	6%	4%	12%	17%	16%	41%
Weekly attendance	0%	0%	0%	1%	1%	5%	4%	9%	16%	20%	44%
Monthly attendance	0%	1%	1%	1%	1%	6%	5%	15%	16%	23%	31%
Less than monthly attendance	4%	1%	1%	1%	1%	10%	6%	16%	25%	13%	24%
Leaders	1%	0%	0%	0%	1%	4%	2%	9%	18%	23%	42%
Non-leaders	1%	1%	1%	1%	1%	8%	7%	14%	18%	16%	32%

n=1,003 U.S. churched adults, September 16–October 4, 2021.

Spiritual Formation
Thriving Churches

In Barna's research of thriving churches, the "spiritual formation" dimension looks at how a church partners with congregants in growing their faith.

Churched Adults on Spiritual Formation & Their Church

"This church is an essential partner in my spiritual formation."

● 0 Disagree strongly ● 1 ● 2 ● 3 ● 4 ● 5 ● 6 ● 7 ● 8 ● 9 ● 10 Agree strongly

	0	1	2	3	4	5	6	7	8	9	10
All churched adults	1%	0	1%	1%	1%	5%	6%	9%	17%	19%	39%
Church tenure (2 or fewer years)	1%	0%	1%	1%	2%	7%	6%	12%	21%	18%	30%
Church tenure (3–10 years)	1%	0%	1%	1%	1%	3%	6%	10%	17%	23%	36%
Church tenure (10+ years)	1%	0%	0%	1%	0%	6%	5%	7%	14%	17%	48%
Weekly attendance	1%	0%	0%	1%	0%	5%	4%	7%	14%	19%	49%
Monthly attendance	0%	0%	1%	1%	2%	4%	6%	11%	18%	24%	32%
Less than monthly attendance	3%	1%	1%	2%	3%	7%	10%	14%	23%	15%	21%
Leaders	1%	0%	0%	0%	1%	3%	4%	7%	16%	24%	43%
Non-leaders	1%	0%	1%	2%	1%	6%	8%	11%	18%	16%	35%

U.S. Churched Adults' Spiritual Formation Score

81
Out of 100

Levels of Spiritual Formation

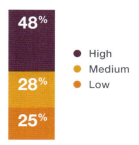

48% High
28% Medium
25% Low

Churched Adults on Next Steps for Spiritual Growth

"My next steps for spiritual growth at this church are clear to me."

● 0 Disagree strongly ● 1 ● 2 ● 3 ● 4 ● 5 ● 6 ● 7 ● 8 ● 9 ● 10 Agree strongly

Group	0	1	2	3	4	5	6	7	8	9	10
All churched adults	1%	0%	1%	1%	2%	9%	6%	12%	18%	19%	30%
Church tenure (2 or fewer years)	1%	1%	1%	2%	3%	9%	7%	16%	16%	19%	26%
Church tenure (3–10 years)	1%	0%	2%	1%	2%	8%	4%	13%	19%	22%	29%
Church tenure (10+ years)	2%	0%	0%	1%	2%	12%	7%	10%	17%	16%	34%
Weekly attendance	0%	0%	1%	1%	2%	10%	5%	10%	16%	16%	37%
Monthly attendance	1%	0%	1%	2%	2%	8%	5%	12%	18%	27%	24%
Less than monthly attendance	3%	1%	1%	1%	2%	11%	11%	18%	20%	15%	18%
Leaders	0%	0%	0%	1%	1%	5%	4%	10%	16%	25%	38%
Non-leaders	2%	1%	1%	2%	3%	12%	8%	14%	19%	14%	24%

n=1,003 U.S. churched adults, September 16–October 4, 2021.

Trusted Leadership
Thriving Churches

In Barna's research of thriving churches, the "trusted leadership" dimension explores the level of trust in church leadership and the clarity of church communication.

Churched Adults on Trusting Leadership

"I have great trust in the leaders of this church."

● 0 Disagree strongly ● 1 ● 2 ● 3 ● 4 ● 5 ● 6 ● 7 ● 8 ● 9 ● 10 Agree strongly

	0	1	2	3	4	5	6	7	8	9	10
All churched adults	1%	0%	1%	1%	1%	6%	5%	9%	20%	18%	39%
Church tenure (2 or fewer years)	1%	0%	1%	0%	3%	8%	6%	13%	18%	17%	32%
Church tenure (3–10 years)	1%	1%	1%	1%	1%	4%	3%	10%	22%	20%	38%
Church tenure (10+ years)	1%	0%	1%	1%	0%	6%	5%	5%	18%	16%	45%
Weekly attendance	0%	0%	1%	0%	0%	5%	3%	6%	19%	16%	48%
Monthly attendance	0%	1%	1%	0%	3%	5%	4%	9%	18%	24%	34%
Less than monthly attendance	3%	0%	1%	1%	2%	9%	9%	15%	22%	14%	23%
Leaders	0%	0%	0%	0%	1%	4%	4%	9%	17%	21%	43%
Non-leaders	2%	1%	2%	1%	1%	7%	5%	9%	22%	15%	36%

U.S. Churched Adults' Trusted Leadership Score

85
Out of 100

Levels of Trust in Leaders

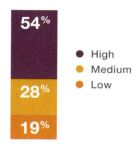

54% — ● High
28% — ● Medium
19% — ● Low

Churched Adults on Church Communication

"Communication from this church is clear."

● 0 Disagree strongly ● 1 ● 2 ● 3 ● 4 ● 5 ● 6 ● 7 ● 8 ● 9 ● 10 Agree strongly

	0	1	2	3	4	5	6	7	8	9	10
All churched adults	0%	0%	1%	1%	1%	4%	4%	11%	19%	18%	42%
Church tenure (2 or fewer years)	0%	1%	0%	0%	2%	5%	7%	11%	22%	17%	35%
Church tenure (3–10 years)	0%	0%	1%	1%	1%	3%	3%	12%	20%	21%	39%
Church tenure (10+ years)	0%	0%	1%	1%	0%	4%	4%	9%	15%	17%	50%
Weekly attendance	0%	0%	1%	0%	1%	3%	3%	6%	17%	18%	50%
Monthly attendance	0%	1%	1%	1%	0%	4%	3%	11%	17%	21%	42%
Less than monthly attendance	1%	1%	0%	1%	2%	5%	9%	21%	25%	14%	20%
Leaders	0%	0%	0%	0%	1%	2%	3%	6%	19%	22%	46%
Non-leaders	1%	1%	1%	1%	1%	5%	5%	14%	18%	15%	38%

n=1,003 U.S. churched adults, September 16–October 4, 2021.

Faith-Sharing
Thriving Churches

In Barna's research of thriving churches, the "faith-sharing" dimension looks at how a church is equipping and encouraging congregants to talk about and share their faith in Jesus.

Churched Adults on Being Encouraged to Share Their Faith

"The congregation is encouraged to talk about their faith in Jesus with others."

● 0 Disagree strongly ● 1 ● 2 ● 3 ● 4 ● 5 ● 6 ● 7 ● 8 ● 9 ● 10 Agree strongly

	0	1	2	3	4	5	6	7	8	9	10
All churched adults	1%	0	0%	1%	1%	6%	5%	10%	18%	17%	40%
Church tenure (2 or fewer years)	1%	0	0%	1%	2%	7%	5%	11%	22%	15%	34%
Church tenure (3–10 years)	0%	0%	0%	1%	1%	3%	6%	9%	18%	22%	40%
Church tenure (10+ years)	1%	0%	1%	1%	0%	7%	3%	11%	15%	15%	45%
Weekly attendance	0%	0%	0%	1%	1%	5%	2%	9%	18%	18%	46%
Monthly attendance	1%	0%	0%	1%	1%	5%	5%	12%	17%	20%	38%
Less than monthly attendance	2%	0%	1%	0%	1%	8%	11%	13%	22%	11%	29%
Leaders	0%	0%	0%	0%	1%	4%	2%	7%	20%	21%	44%
Non-leaders	1%	0%	1%	2%	1%	7%	7%	13%	18%	15%	37%

U.S. Churched Adults' Faith-Sharing Score

80
Out of 100

Levels of Faith-Sharing

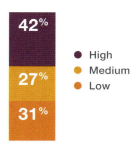

42% ● High
27% ● Medium
31% ● Low

Churched Adults on Feeling Equipped to Share Their Faith

"I feel fully equipped to share my faith with people who do not attend church."

● 0 Disagree strongly   ● 1   ● 2   ● 3   ● 4   ● 5   ● 6   ● 7   ● 8   ● 9   ● 10 Agree strongly

	0	1	2	3	4	5	6	7	8	9	10
All churched adults	3%	1%	1%	3%	2%	9%	7%	14%	17%	14%	29%
Church tenure (2 or fewer years)	3%	1%	1%	3%	1%	8%	6%	17%	19%	16%	25%
Church tenure (3–10 years)	2%	2%	0%	3%	2%	6%	9%	12%	18%	14%	30%
Church tenure (10+ years)	3%	0%	2%	3%	3%	12%	7%	12%	14%	13%	31%
Weekly attendance	2%	1%	1%	3%	2%	10%	6%	10%	16%	15%	34%
Monthly attendance	1%	1%	0%	4%	2%	8%	10%	17%	15%	17%	26%
Less than monthly attendance	6%	0%	1%	3%	4%	8%	8%	17%	22%	10%	21%
Leaders	1%	0%	0%	1%	1%	5%	5%	10%	18%	21%	37%
Non-leaders	4%	2%	2%	4%	3%	12%	9%	16%	16%	9%	23%

n=1,003 U.S. churched adults, September 16–October 4, 2021.

Serving Others
Thriving Churches

In Barna's research of thriving churches, the "serving others" dimension measures how a church is empowering congregants to make an impact and whether congregants are taking time to serve.

Churched Adults on Serving Others

"I give away my time to serve and help others in my community."

● 0 Disagree strongly ● 1 ● 2 ● 3 ● 4 ● 5 ● 6 ● 7 ● 8 ● 9 ● 10 Agree strongly

All churched adults

0	1	2	3	4	5	6	7	8	9	10
3%	1%	1%	2%	2%	9%	7%	13%	19%	16%	27%

Church tenure (2 or fewer years)

0	1	2	3	4	5	6	7	8	9	10
2%	2%	2%	2%	2%	9%	5%	15%	17%	18%	27%

Church tenure (3–10 years)

0	1	2	3	4	5	6	7	8	9	10
3%	1%	1%	1%	2%	7%	7%	13%	22%	16%	28%

Church tenure (10+ years)

0	1	2	3	4	5	6	7	8	9	10
3%	1%	1%	3%	3%	12%	8%	12%	17%	13%	27%

Weekly attendance

0	1	2	3	4	5	6	7	8	9	10
3%	1%	1%	2%	2%	9%	5%	12%	17%	17%	31%

Monthly attendance

0	1	2	3	4	5	6	7	8	9	10
3%	1%	1%	2%	1%	9%	10%	14%	17%	15%	26%

Less than monthly attendance

0	1	2	3	4	5	6	7	8	9	10
3%	1%	1%	1%	5%	8%	6%	16%	26%	13%	20%

Leaders

0	1	2	3	4	5	6	7	8	9	10
0%	0%	0%	1%	1%	4%	3%	9%	21%	23%	38%

Non-leaders

0	1	2	3	4	5	6	7	8	9	10
5%	2%	2%	2%	3%	13%	10%	16%	17%	10%	19%

U.S. Churched Adults' Serving Others Score

79

Out of 100

Levels of Serving Others

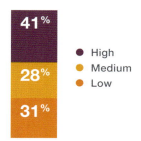

41% High
28% Medium
31% Low

Churched Adults on Feeling Empowered

"This church empowers me to make an impact in the lives of others."

● 0 Disagree strongly   ● 1   ● 2   ● 3   ● 4   ● 5   ● 6   ● 7   ● 8   ● 9   ● 10 Agree strongly

	0	1	2	3	4	5	6	7	8	9	10
All churched adults	1%	0%	1%	1%	2%	6%	7%	11%	18%	20%	35%
Church tenure (2 or fewer years)	2%	0%	1%	0%	3%	6%	8%	12%	20%	17%	31%
Church tenure (3–10 years)	1%	1%	1%	1%	1%	5%	6%	10%	16%	23%	35%
Church tenure (10+ years)	1%	0%	0%	1%	2%	7%	6%	10%	18%	18%	37%
Weekly attendance	1%	0%	0%	1%	1%	6%	5%	9%	17%	20%	41%
Monthly attendance	1%	0%	0%	1%	1%	5%	8%	10%	19%	23%	31%
Less than monthly attendance	3%	1%	1%	0%	4%	8%	10%	16%	19%	15%	22%
Leaders	0%	0%	0%	0%	2%	3%	4%	9%	15%	25%	42%
Non-leaders	2%	0%	1%	1%	2%	9%	9%	12%	20%	16%	29%

n=1,003 U.S. churched adults, September 16–October 4, 2021.

Social Impact
Thriving Churches

In Barna's research of thriving churches, the "social impact" dimension measures how a church addresses injustice and provides opportunities for congregants to do so.

Churched Adults on Their Church Addressing Injustice

"This church is involved in addressing injustices in society."

Legend: ● 0 Disagree strongly ● 1 ● 2 ● 3 ● 4 ● 5 ● 6 ● 7 ● 8 ● 9 ● 10 Agree strongly

	0	1	2	3	4	5	6	7	8	9	10
All churched adults	2%	1%	1%	1%	2%	11%	7%	13%	18%	16%	29%
Church tenure (2 or fewer years)	2%	1%	0%	1%	2%	11%	8%	13%	20%	14%	29%
Church tenure (3–10 years)	1%	1%	2%	1%	2%	8%	5%	14%	20%	19%	27%
Church tenure (10+ years)	3%	1%	0%	1%	1%	14%	8%	13%	15%	14%	30%
Weekly attendance	2%	0%	1%	1%	2%	11%	5%	12%	17%	16%	32%
Monthly attendance	0%	1%	1%	1%	2%	10%	8%	13%	20%	15%	28%
Less than monthly attendance	3%	1%	0%	1%	1%	13%	9%	19%	19%	14%	20%
Leaders	1%	1%	1%	0%	1%	6%	4%	10%	18%	21%	38%
Non-leaders	2%	1%	1%	1%	3%	15%	9%	16%	19%	12%	21%

U.S. Churched Adults' Social Impact Score

79
Out of 100

Levels of Social Impact

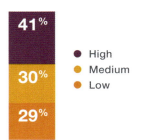

41% — ● High
30% — ● Medium
29% — ● Low

Churched Adults on Opportunities to Help

"This church provides opportunities for me to help those who are suffering or marginalized."

● 0 Disagree strongly ● 1 ● 2 ● 3 ● 4 ● 5 ● 6 ● 7 ● 8 ● 9 ● 10 Agree strongly

	0	1	2	3	4	5	6	7	8	9	10
All churched adults	1%	1%	1%	1%	2%	7%	5%	13%	20%	19%	31%
Church tenure (2 or fewer years)	1%	1%	1%	1%	3%	8%	5%	13%	20%	20%	28%
Church tenure (3–10 years)	0%	0%	1%	1%	1%	5%	4%	14%	19%	21%	33%
Church tenure (10+ years)	1%	1%	0%	1%	1%	7%	7%	11%	22%	17%	31%
Weekly attendance	1%	0%	1%	1%	1%	8%	4%	10%	20%	19%	35%
Monthly attendance	1%	0%	0%	1%	2%	3%	7%	14%	18%	22%	30%
Less than monthly attendance	1%	2%	0%	0%	2%	8%	6%	19%	25%	17%	20%
Leaders	1%	0%	0%	0%	2%	3%	3%	10%	19%	22%	41%
Non-leaders	1%	1%	1%	2%	1%	9%	8%	15%	22%	17%	23%

n=1,003 U.S. churched adults, September 16–October 4, 2021.

Holistic Stewardship
Thriving Churches

In Barna's research of thriving churches, the "holistic stewardship" dimension measures how well a church is helping congregants embrace their calling and use their gifts.

Churched Adults on Using Their Gifts to Serve

"This church helps me find ways to use all of my gifts (time, skills and financial resources) to honor God and serve others."

● 0 Disagree strongly ● 1 ● 2 ● 3 ● 4 ● 5 ● 6 ● 7 ● 8 ● 9 ● 10 Agree strongly

	0	1	2	3	4	5	6	7	8	9	10
All churched adults	1%	1%	1%	1%	1%	7%	6%	11%	21%	18%	33%
Church tenure (2 or fewer years)	1%	1%	1%	0%	3%	9%	7%	9%	21%	15%	32%
Church tenure (3–10 years)	1%	0%	1%	2%	1%	5%	6%	12%	20%	20%	33%
Church tenure (10+ years)	1%	0%	0%	2%	0%	7%	5%	10%	22%	17%	35%
Weekly attendance	1%	0%	1%	1%	1%	7%	3%	8%	19%	19%	41%
Monthly attendance	1%	1%	0%	2%	2%	4%	7%	15%	21%	18%	29%
Less than monthly attendance	3%	1%	2%	0%	2%	10%	11%	13%	24%	14%	21%
Leaders	0%	0%	0%	0%	1%	4%	3%	7%	21%	20%	42%
Non-leaders	2%	1%	1%	2%	1%	9%	8%	13%	21%	15%	27%

U.S. Churched Adults' Holistic Stewardship Score

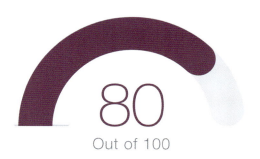

80 Out of 100

Levels of Holistic Stewardship

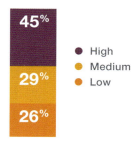

- 45% ● High
- 29% ● Medium
- 26% ● Low

Churched Adults on Embracing Their Calling

"This church has helped me embrace my calling in life."

● 0 Disagree strongly ● 1 ● 2 ● 3 ● 4 ● 5 ● 6 ● 7 ● 8 ● 9 ● 10 Agree strongly

	0	1	2	3	4	5	6	7	8	9	10
All churched adults	1%	1%	1%	2%	3%	7%	7%	10%	18%	18%	32%
Church tenure (2 or fewer years)	1%	2%	1%	2%	3%	8%	7%	15%	16%	17%	29%
Church tenure (3–10 years)	1%	1%	1%	1%	2%	6%	8%	8%	21%	20%	31%
Church tenure (10+ years)	2%	1%	0%	1%	3%	9%	7%	8%	17%	17%	36%
Weekly attendance	1%	0%	1%	1%	3%	8%	5%	7%	17%	19%	38%
Monthly attendance	1%	2%	1%	2%	1%	6%	8%	14%	18%	20%	28%
Less than monthly attendance	3%	3%	0%	2%	3%	9%	12%	12%	21%	13%	21%
Leaders	0%	0%	0%	1%	2%	4%	5%	8%	17%	23%	42%
Non-leaders	2%	2%	1%	2%	4%	10%	9%	12%	19%	14%	24%

n=1,003 U.S. churched adults, September 16–October 4, 2021.

Leadership Development
Thriving Churches

In Barna's research of thriving churches, the "leadership development" dimension looks at how a church is preparing individuals, especially in the next generation, for leadership.

Churched Adults on Training Pathways in Their Church

"There is a clear training pathway for developing leaders in this church."

● 0 Disagree strongly　● 1　● 2　● 3　● 4　● 5　● 6　● 7　● 8　● 9　● 10 Agree strongly

Group	0	1	2	3	4	5	6	7	8	9	10
All churched adults	1%	0%	1%	2%	2%	8%	7%	11%	20%	18%	30%
Church tenure (2 or fewer years)	1%	0%	0%	2%	3%	8%	7%	13%	18%	19%	29%
Church tenure (3–10 years)	1%	0%	1%	2%	1%	5%	8%	12%	21%	19%	30%
Church tenure (10+ years)	1%	0%	2%	1%	1%	11%	8%	9%	19%	15%	32%
Weekly attendance	1%	0%	1%	2%	2%	9%	4%	9%	20%	18%	34%
Monthly attendance	1%	0%	1%	2%	0%	7%	9%	13%	18%	19%	31%
Less than monthly attendance	3%	1%	1%	2%	2%	7%	15%	16%	22%	14%	19%
Leaders	0%	0%	0%	1%	1%	5%	5%	6%	22%	23%	37%
Non-leaders	2%	0%	1%	3%	2%	11%	9%	15%	18%	13%	25%

U.S. Churched Adults' Leadership Development Score

80
Out of 100

Levels of Leadership Development

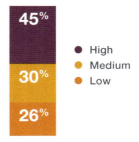

45% ● High
30% ● Medium
26% ● Low

Churched Adults on Empowering Young Leaders

"This church empowers young people to become leaders."

● 0 Disagree strongly ● 1 ● 2 ● 3 ● 4 ● 5 ● 6 ● 7 ● 8 ● 9 ● 10 Agree strongly

	0	1	2	3	4	5	6	7	8	9	10
All churched adults	1%	0%	1%	1%	2%	7%	8%	11%	18%	18%	34%
Church tenure (2 or fewer years)	1%	0%	1%	1%	1%	8%	9%	14%	20%	13%	32%
Church tenure (3–10 years)	0%	0%	1%	0%	2%	5%	8%	8%	19%	24%	32%
Church tenure (10+ years)	1%	0%	2%	1%	2%	8%	7%	12%	16%	15%	36%
Weekly attendance	0%	0%	1%	1%	2%	7%	5%	10%	19%	18%	37%
Monthly attendance	1%	0%	2%	1%	1%	5%	10%	11%	16%	20%	34%
Less than monthly attendance	2%	0%	2%	1%	1%	9%	12%	17%	20%	13%	24%
Leaders	0%	0%	1%	0%	1%	3%	5%	8%	21%	20%	41%
Non-leaders	1%	0%	2%	2%	2%	10%	10%	14%	16%	16%	28%

n=1,003 U.S. churched adults, September 16–October 4, 2021.

Future-Focused
Thriving Churches

In Barna's research of thriving churches, the "future-focused" dimension assesses a church's clarity of vision and the priority they place on the next generation. *This question is only asked of churched adults who say they have a leadership position in their church. This could be a wide variety of roles, including deacons, elders, volunteer coordinators, team leaders, committee members, etc.*

Church Leaders on the Next Generation

"The next genereation is essential to the future of this church."

	0 Disagree strongly	1	2	3	4	5	6	7	8	9	10 Agree strongly
All church leaders	0%	0%	1%	0%	2%	4%	3%	6%	18%	19%	47%
Church tenure (2 or fewer years)	0%	0%	1%	0%	5%	7%	4%	11%	22%	17%	33%
Church tenure (3–10 years)	0%	0%	1%	0%	1%	1%	2%	4%	18%	23%	51%
Church tenure (10+ years)	0%	0%	0%	0%	1%	4%	0%	3%	13%	18%	63%
Weekly attendance	0%	0%	1%	0%	2%	2%	2%	3%	16%	19%	56%
Monthly attendance	0%	0%	0%	0%	1%	4%	3%	10%	16%	24%	41%
Less than monthly attendance	0%	0%	1%	0%	5%	6%	4%	10%	27%	16%	31%

U.S. Church Leaders' Future-Focused Score

87

Out of 100

Levels of Future Focus

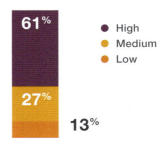

61%
27%
13%

- High
- Medium
- Low

Church Leaders on a Clear Vision

"There is a clear vision for the future of this church."

● 0 Disagree strongly   ● 1   ● 2   ● 3   ● 4   ● 5   ● 6   ● 7   ● 8   ● 9   ● 10 Agree strongly

All church leaders

0%	0%	0%	0%	1%	4%	3%	8%	19%	22%	43%

Church tenure (2 or fewer years)

0%	0%	0%	1%	2%	7%	5%	10%	21%	18%	35%

Church tenure (3–10 years)

0%	0%	0%	0%	0%	1%	2%	8%	17%	30%	42%

Church tenure (10+ years)

0%	0%	1%	0%	0%	5%	2%	5%	18%	16%	54%

Weekly attendance

0%	0%	0%	1%	0%	3%	3%	6%	19%	20%	48%

Monthly attendance

0%	0%	0%	0%	0%	2%	4%	9%	15%	28%	43%

Less than monthly attendance

0%	0%	1%	0%	3%	8%	5%	11%	22%	19%	30%

n=410 U.S. church leaders, September 16–October 4, 2021.

Resource Stability
Thriving Churches

In Barna's research of thriving churches, the "resource stability" dimension looks at a church's financial optimism and confidence in the number of volunteers and leaders. *This question is only asked of churched adults who say they have a leadership position in their church. This could be a wide variety of roles, including deacons, elders, volunteer coordinators, team leaders, committee members, etc.*

Church Leaders on the Financial Stability of Their Church

"I am optimistic about the financial stability of this church going forward."

● 0 Disagree strongly ● 1 ● 2 ● 3 ● 4 ● 5 ● 6 ● 7 ● 8 ● 9 ● 10 Agree strongly

	0	1	2	3	4	5	6	7	8	9	10
All church leaders	1%	0%	0%	1%	1%	4%	3%	9%	17%	23%	42%
Church tenure (2 or fewer years)	0%	0%	0%	1%	2%	6%	5%	11%	20%	20%	36%
Church tenure (3–10 years)	0%	0%	0%	0%	0%	2%	1%	10%	14%	32%	41%
Church tenure (10+ years)	2%	0%	0%	1%	1%	5%	2%	4%	16%	16%	54%
Weekly attendance	1%	0%	0%	0%	1%	3%	1%	6%	16%	24%	48%
Monthly attendance	0%	0%	0%	0%	0%	4%	4%	9%	20%	23%	40%
Less than monthly attendance	0%	0%	0%	2%	2%	6%	5%	16%	15%	23%	31%

U.S. Church Leaders' Resource Stability Score

86
Out of 100

Levels of Resource Stability

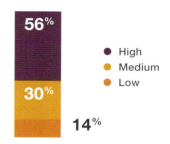

56%
30%
14%

● High
● Medium
● Low

Church Leaders on Volunteers in Their Church

"This church has enough leaders and volunteers to operate effectively."

● 0 Disagree strongly   ● 1   ● 2   ● 3   ● 4   ● 5   ● 6   ● 7   ● 8   ● 9   ● 10 Agree strongly

	0	1	2	3	4	5	6	7	8	9	10
All church leaders	0%	0%	0%	1%	1%	5%	4%	12%	19%	17%	41%
Church tenure (2 or fewer years)	0%	0%	1%	1%	1%	7%	5%	11%	19%	18%	37%
Church tenure (3–10 years)	0%	0%	0%	1%	1%	1%	3%	14%	19%	18%	42%
Church tenure (10+ years)	0%	0%	0%	0%	1%	6%	4%	9%	21%	12%	47%
Weekly attendance	0%	0%	0%	0%	2%	4%	3%	12%	19%	15%	45%
Monthly attendance	0%	0%	0%	1%	1%	4%	2%	13%	18%	20%	41%
Less than monthly attendance	0%	0%	1%	1%	0%	6%	8%	10%	23%	17%	34%

n=410 U.S. church leaders, September 16–October 4, 2021.

Team Health
Thriving Churches

In Barna's research of thriving churches, the "team health" dimension looks at the clarity of roles and level of internal trust among leadership in a church. *This question is only asked of churched adults who say they have a leadership position in their church. This could be a wide variety of roles, including deacons, elders, volunteer coordinators, team leaders, committee members, etc.*

Church Leaders on the Expectations of Their Role

"I am clear about the expectations of my role."

● 0 Disagree strongly ● 1 ● 2 ● 3 ● 4 ● 5 ● 6 ● 7 ● 8 ● 9 ● 10 Agree strongly

	0	1	2	3	4	5	6	7	8	9	10
All church leaders	0%	0%	0%	1%	0%	3%	4%	9%	19%	21%	42%
Church tenure (2 or fewer years)	0%	0%	0%	2%	1%	5%	7%	10%	22%	20%	33%
Church tenure (3–10 years)	0%	0%	0%	1%	0%	1%	3%	8%	19%	26%	41%
Church tenure (10+ years)	0%	0%	0%	1%	0%	3%	1%	7%	17%	16%	55%
Weekly attendance	0%	0%	0%	1%	0%	3%	2%	4%	18%	22%	50%
Monthly attendance	0%	0%	0%	1%	1%	1%	6%	11%	22%	21%	37%
Less than monthly attendance	0%	0%	0%	2%	0%	6%	8%	17%	20%	20%	28%

U.S. Church Leaders' Team Health Score

88
Out of 100

Levels of Team Health

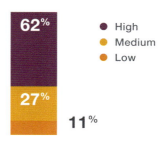

- High
- Medium
- Low

62%
27%
11%

Church Leaders on Trust

How would you rate the trust between church leaders internally?

● 0 Poor ● 1 ● 2 ● 3 ● 4 ● 5 ● 6 ● 7 ● 8 ● 9 ● 10 Excellent

	0	1	2	3	4	5	6	7	8	9	10
All church leaders	0%	0%	0%	0%	1%	3%	3%	8%	18%	21%	45%
Church tenure (2 or fewer years)	0%	0%	0%	0%	2%	7%	6%	10%	20%	19%	36%
Church tenure (3–10 years)	0%	1%	0%	1%	0%	1%	2%	6%	18%	26%	46%
Church tenure (10+ years)	0%	0%	0%	1%	0%	2%	1%	6%	16%	19%	56%
Weekly attendance	0%	0%	0%	0%	0%	2%	2%	6%	17%	24%	49%
Monthly attendance	0%	0%	0%	1%	1%	2%	4%	9%	15%	20%	48%
Less than monthly attendance	0%	1%	0%	0%	3%	7%	5%	10%	26%	17%	32%

n=410 U.S. church leaders, September 16–October 4, 2021.

Data-Informed
Thriving Churches

In Barna's research of thriving churches, the "data-informed" dimension assesses whether a church has systems in place to know and track attendees and make well-informed decisions. *This question is only asked of churched adults who say they have a leadership position in their church. This could be a wide variety of roles, including deacons, elders, volunteer coordinators, team leaders, committee members, etc.*

Church Leaders on Being Data-Informed

"As a leader, I have the data I need to make well-informed ministry decisions."

● 0 Disagree strongly ● 1 ● 2 ● 3 ● 4 ● 5 ● 6 ● 7 ● 8 ● 9 ● 10 Agree strongly

	0	1	2	3	4	5	6	7	8	9	10
All church leaders	1%	0%	0%	0%	2%	3%	3%	9%	19%	21%	42%
Church tenure (2 or fewer years)	0%	0%	1%	1%	2%	4%	5%	9%	23%	17%	38%
Church tenure (3–10 years)	1%	0%	0%	0%	2%	2%	1%	11%	16%	23%	44%
Church tenure (10+ years)	4%	0%	0%	0%	3%	0%	4%	4%	18%	23%	44%
Weekly attendance	2%	0%	0%	0%	1%	1%	2%	6%	16%	23%	48%
Monthly attendance	1%	0%	0%	0%	5%	2%	4%	6%	19%	24%	39%
Less than monthly attendance	0%	0%	1%	0%	3%	6%	4%	17%	27%	12%	30%

U.S. Church Leaders' Data-Informed Score

86
Out of 100

Levels of Data-Informed Leadership

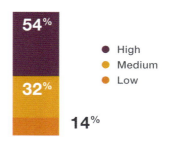

54%

32%

14%

● High
● Medium
● Low

Church Leaders on Knowing Their People

"We have good systems in place to know and track our people."

● 0 Disagree strongly ● 1 ● 2 ● 3 ● 4 ● 5 ● 6 ● 7 ● 8 ● 9 ● 10 Agree strongly

All church leaders

| 1% | 0% | 0% | 0% | 1% | 4% | 5% | 9% | 21% | 24% | 36% |

Church tenure (2 or fewer years)

| 0% | 0% | 0% | 0% | 1% | 7% | 5% | 10% | 25% | 18% | 32% |

Church tenure (3–10 years)

| 0% | 1% | 1% | 0% | 0% | 1% | 3% | 8% | 18% | 34% | 33% |

Church tenure (10+ years)

| 2% | 0% | 0% | 1% | 2% | 3% | 5% | 7% | 19% | 16% | 46% |

Weekly attendance

| 1% | 0% | 0% | 0% | 1% | 3% | 3% | 6% | 21% | 23% | 40% |

Monthly attendance

| 0% | 0% | 1% | 0% | 1% | 4% | 7% | 8% | 20% | 26% | 34% |

Less than monthly attendance

| 0% | 0% | 0% | 0% | 0% | 7% | 7% | 15% | 21% | 22% | 28% |

n=410 U.S. church leaders, September 16–October 4, 2021.

Methodology

The studies of human flourishing and thriving churches referenced in this book were conducted by Barna Group among a nationally representative sample of the population identified. Barna used online data collection through national consumer panels. Respondents were fully verified by the consumer panels and representative sample sources. Additionally, quality control measures checked that respondents were completing surveys at an appropriate pace and paying attention to the questions asked. Quotas were set to obtain a minimum readable sample by a variety of demographic factors, and analysts weighted the samples by region, ethnicity, education, age and gender to reflect their natural presence in the American population (using U.S. Census Bureau data for comparison). Partly by nature of using an online panel, these respondents are slightly more educated than the average American, but Barna researchers adjusted the representation of college-educated individuals in the weighting scheme accordingly.

Sample Size	Audience	Dates Conducted	Sample Error (at 95% confidence level)
1,093	U.S. adults	November 11–19, 2019	+ / - 2.8%
1,000	U.S. adults	April 28–May 5, 2020	+ / - 2.9%
1,003	U.S. churched adults	September 16–October 4, 2021	+ / - 3.1%

Glossary

- **Churched adults:** U.S. adults who have attended a church service in person or online on average at least once every six months over the last year (excluding holiday services, such as Christmas or Easter, or special events like weddings and funerals). For the September 16–October 4, 2021 survey, churched adults must also say they have a "primary" church; they were asked to think about their primary church as they scored the various dimensions of thriving.

- **Practicing Christians:** U.S. self-identified Christians who say their religious faith is very important in their lives today and have attended a church service in-person or online on average at least one time per month over the last year.

- **Resilient disciples:** U.S. self-identified Christians who 1) attend church at least monthly and engage with their church more than just attending worship services; 2) trust firmly in the authority of the Bible; 3) are committed to Jesus personally and affirm he was crucified and raised from the dead to conquer sin and death; and 4) express desire to transform the broader society as an outcome of their faith.

- **Four-point evangelicals:** U.S. adults who 1) believe they will go to heaven because they have confessed their sins and accepted Jesus as their savior; 2) strongly believe the Bible is accurate in the principles it teaches; 3) strongly believe they have a personal responsibility to share their faith with others and 4) strongly disagree that a person can earn their way into heaven through good works.

- **Generations**
  - » Gen Z: born between 1999 and 2015
  - » Millennials: born between 1984 and 1998
  - » Gen X: born between 1965 and 1983
  - » Boomers: born between 1946 and 1964
  - » Elders: born in 1945 or earlier

- **Church leaders:** churched adults who respond "yes" to the following question: At your church, do you hold some kind of leadership position? This could be a wide variety of roles, including deacons, elders, volunteer coordinators, team leaders, committee members, etc.

- **Levels of Flourishing and Thriving**
  - » High: percentage of respondents who provide a score of nine or 10 (on a scale of zero to 10) for both items within a flourishing or thriving dimension. *This grouping is commonly referred to as those who "give high scores" within a dimension, or they may be called "flourishing" in this dimension.*
  - » Medium: percentage of respondents who provide a score of seven or eight (on a scale of zero to 10) for both items within a flourishing or thriving dimension.
  - » Low: respondents who score at least one of the two items in a flourishing or thriving dimension as a six or lower (on a scale of zero to 10).

- **Flourishing and Thriving Scores:** Researchers added together the average numerical scores of the two items within each dimension. As each item was scored on a scale of zero to 10, this sum could have been any value on a scale of zero to 20. Researchers then multiplied this sum by five, creating a score on a scale of zero to 100.

Field Guide Insights

To collect recommendations for the field guide sections, Barna and Gloo identified a number of churches who have made effort to use data in their ministry decisions. These include several churches of varying sizes and denominations that took place in Barna CoLabs, took assessments through Barna or Gloo or otherwise stood out as having made intentional decisions to learn about or embrace data-informed ministry. A practitioner from each church participated in a "case study" interview or Q&A to share more about their experiences and provide insights for other pastors and leaders on a journey to measure what matters.

Acknowledgments

First and foremost, Barna Group thanks our partners at Gloo, led by Scott Beck, for their support—in conducting research on flourishing people and thriving churches, building the ChurchPulse assessment, producing this book and helping us leverage data and serve the Church with new technology and tools. Our work and our team have been steadied through the turbulence of recent years by Gloo's generosity, spirit of collaboration and commitment to excellence. So many names could be listed and thanked across our shared initiatives. For now, we especially want to express appreciation to the following individuals who were instrumental in the production of this research and book: Esther Ball-Babois, Rachel Finley, Matt Fischer, Dr. Jeff Fray, Linda Glaze, Brad Hill, Devon Kline, Dr. Peter Larson, Dr. Nancy Scammacca Lewis, Linda Peirce, Samuel Shew, Raman Sinha, Cheyanne Skeldon, Matt Smay, Nancy Smith, Krista Stadler, Dillon Wilson and Travis Young.

The Barna research team included Daniel Copeland, Aidan Dunn, Brooke Hempell, Pam Jacob, Savannah Kimberlin, David Kinnaman and Traci Stark (with great partnership with Drs. Fray, Larson and Lewis at Gloo on assessment development). Ashley Ekmay and Chanté Smith assisted with data collection and verification. Alyce Youngblood produced the manuscript with support from Cicely Corry, Kimberlin and Verónica Thames. Lauren Petersen produced and adapted extended interviews. Doug Brown provided support with copy edits and proofreading. With creative direction from Joe Jensen, OX Creative designed the cover. Annette Allen designed infographics. Rob Williams and Brenda Usery designed interior pages and data visualizations. Usery managed production overall, and Elissa Clouse, Mallory Holt and T'nea Rolle coordinated as project managers at various phases of the project.

Additional thanks for the support of our Barna colleagues through this season and in the broader State of Your Church initiative: Amy Brands, Jeni Cohen, Juli Cooper, Mel Grabendike, Aly Hawkins, Dr. Charlotte Marshall Powell, Steve McBeth, Matt Randerson, Layla Shahmohammadi and Todd White.

Many pastors, experts, authors and scholars helped bring the research to life and provided practical recommendations for measuring what matters.

Specifically, Barna thanks the contributors featured in these pages: Claude Alexander, Ryan Burge, Brian Carson, Mark Chaves, Jenni Clayville, Kadi Cole, Nancy Duarte, Randy Frazee, Tara Beth Leach, Toni Mihal, Glenn Packiam, Brianna Parker, Nicholas Pearce, John Perez, Scott Sauls, Ed Stetzer, Chris Thayer, Drew Van Culin, Tyler VanderWeele and Ashley Wilcox.

Endnotes

1. See Matthew 9:14–17, Mark 2:18–22 and Luke 5:33–39
2. Frederick Buechner, *Wishful Thinking: A Seeker's ABC* (San Francisco: HarperOne, 1993).
3. Jonathan Sacks, "Light in Dark Times," 2014, https://www.rabbisacks.org/covenant-conversation/vayetse/light-in-dark-times/.
4. Barna Group, "38% of U.S. Pastors Have Thought About Quitting Full-Time Ministry in the Past Year," November 16, 2021, https://www.barna.com/research/pastors-well-being/.
5. Arlie Hoschild, *The Managed Heart: Commercialization of Human Feeling* (Berkeley: University of California Press, 1983).
6. Rick Hellman, "How to Make Friends? Study Reveals It Takes Time," University of Kansas News Service, March 28, 2018, https://news.ku.edu/2018/03/06/study-reveals-number-hours-it-takes-make-friend.
7. Frederick Buechner, *The Final Beast* (New York: Atheneum, 1965).
8. The Human Flourishing Program, Institute for Quantitative Social Science, "Our Flourishing Measure," Harvard University, n.d., https://hfh.fas.harvard.edu/measuring-flourishing.
9. Tyler J. VanderWeele and Brendan Case, "Empty Pews Are an American Public Health Crisis," *Christianity Today*, October 19, 2021, https://www.christianitytoday.com/ct/2021/november/church-empty-pews-are-american-public-health-crisis.html.
10. Tyler J. VanderWeele, "Religious Communities and Human Flourishing," *Current Directions in Psychological Science* 26(5) 2017, https://journals.sagepub.com/doi/pdf/10.1177/0963721417721526.
11. David W. Bebbington, *The Evangelical Quadrilateral*, Vol. 1, (Waco, TX: Baylor UP, 2021).
12. Barna Group, *Growing Together* (Ventura, CA: Barna Group, 2022).
13. Barna Group, "Only One-Third of Young Adults Feels Cared for by Others," October 15, 2019, https://www.barna.com/research/global-connection-isolation/.
14. Barna Group, *Restoring Relationships* (Ventura, CA: Barna Group, 2020) 25.
15. Barna Group, "31% of U.S. Adults Report Feeling Lonely at Least Some of Each Day," December 8, 2021, https://www.barna.com/research/mettes-lonely-americans/.
16. Barna Group, *Households of Faith* (Ventura, CA: Barna Group, 2019) 28.
17. Barna Group, "Strong Relationships Within Church Add to Resilient Faith in Young Adults," August 26, 2020, https://www.barna.com/research/relationships-build-resilient-faith/.
18. Barna, *Restoring Relationships*, 85.
19. Bryce Covert, "8 Hours a Day, 5 Days a Week Is Not Working for Us," *The New York Times*, July 20, 2021, https://www.nytimes.com/2021/07/20/opinion/covid-return-to-office.html.
20. Matt Carmichael, "Americans Remain Divided in Attitudes About the Office, and Returning to It," June 30, 2021, Ipsos, https://www.ipsos.com/en-us/news-polls/Americans-remain-divided-in-attitudes-about-the-office-and-returning-to-it.
21. Barna Group, "One in Five Americans Wants the Church's Direction in Vocational Well-Being," September 15, 2021, https://www.barna.com/research/vocational-well-being/.
22. Barna Group, *Christians at Work*, (Ventura, CA: Barna Group, 2018) 90.
23. Barna Group, *Gifted for More* (Ventura, CA: Barna Group, 2021) 61.
24. Barna Group, *Gen Z Vol. 2* (Ventura, CA: Barna Group, 2021) 12.
25. Barna Group, "ChurchPulse Weekly Conversations: Stephanie Shackelford on Vocational Discipleship," September 23, 2021, https://www.barna.com/research/cpw-shackelford/.
26. Barna Group, "56% of Practicing Christians Believe Understanding Their Calling Is a Solo Journey," September 29, 2021, https://www.barna.com/research/pc-calling/.
27. This data is from an online survey of 433 U.S. Protestant senior pastors, conducted from July 19–August 2, 2021.

28. American Bible Society, *The State of the Bible USA 2021*, ebook (Philadelphia, PA: American Bible Society, 2021).

29. This data is from an online study of 459 U.S. pastors, conducted August 14–September 9, 2021.

30. Barna, *Gen Z Vol. 2*, 10

31. Barna Group, *The Connected Generation* (Ventura, CA: Barna Group, 2019) 48.

32. Barna Group, "Americans Feel Good About Counseling," February 27, 2018, https://www.barna.com/research/americans-feel-good-counseling/.

33. Barna, *Restoring Relationships*, 64.

34. This data is from an online survey of 433 U.S. pastors, conducted July 19–August 2, 2021.

35. Centers for Disease Control and Prevention, "COVID Data Tracker Weekly Summary," Accessed January 20, 2022, https://www.cdc.gov/coronavirus/2019-ncov/covid-data/covidview/index.html.

36. Julianne Holt-Lunstad *et al.*, "Loneliness and Social Isolation as Risk Factors for Mortality: A Meta-Analytic Review," *Perspectives on Psychological Science* 10, 2015, https://scholarsarchive.byu.edu/cgi/viewcontent.cgi?article=3024&context=facpub.

37. Melody McGrath Warnick, "Loneliness: The Shadow Pandemic," *Y Magazine*, Summer 2020, https://magazine.byu.edu/article/loneliness-the-shadow-pandemic/.

38. Scott Keeter, "Many Americans Continue to Experience Mental Health Difficulties as Pandemic Enters Second Year," March 16, 2021, Pew Research Center, https://www.pewresearch.org/fact-tank/2021/03/16/many-americans-continue-to-experience-mental-health-difficulties-as-pandemic-enters-second-year/.

39. Glenn Packiam, *The Resilient Pastor* (Grand Rapids, MI: Backer Books, 2022) 23.

40. Barna Group, "Christian Millennials Are Most Likely to Lean Toward Charismatic Worship," July 23, 2020, https://www.barna.com/research/worship-preferences/.

41. Barna Group, "Silent and Solo: How Americans Pray," August 15, 2017, https://www.barna.com/research/silent-solo-americans-pray/.

42. Barna, "Christian Millennials Are Most Likely."

43. Barna Group, "Almost Half of Practicing Christian Millennials Say Evangelism Is Wrong," February 5, 2019, https://www.barna.com/research/millennials-oppose-evangelism/.

44. Barna, *Gifted for More*, 83.

45. Barna, *The Connected Generation*, 59.

46. Barna, *Gifted for More*, 17.

47. Barna, *Christians at Work*, 44.

48. Barna, *Gen Z Vol. 2*, 33.

49. Barna Group, *The State of Pastors* (Ventura, CA: Barna Group, 2017) 99.

50. Barna, *The State of Pastors*, 45.

51. Barna Group, *Trends in the Black Church* (Ventura, CA: Barna Group, 2021) 123.

52. Packiam, *Resilient Pastor*, 232

53. Barna, *The State of Pastors*, 71.

About the Project Partners

BARNA GROUP is a research firm dedicated to providing actionable insights on faith and culture, with a particular focus on the Christian Church. Since 1984, Barna has conducted more than two million interviews in the course of thousands of studies and has become a go-to source for organizations that want to better understand a complex and changing world from a faith perspective. Barna's clients and partners include a broad range of academic institutions, churches, nonprofits and businesses, such as Alpha, the Templeton Foundation, Fuller Seminary, the Bill and Melinda Gates Foundation, Maclellan Foundation, DreamWorks Animation, Focus Features, Habitat for Humanity, The Navigators, NBC-Universal, the ONE Campaign, Paramount Pictures, the Salvation Army, Walden Media, Sony and World Vision. The firm's studies are frequently quoted by major media outlets such as *The Economist*, BBC, CNN, *USA Today*, the *Wall Street Journal*, Fox News, *The Washington Post*, Huffington Post, *The New York Times* and the *Los Angeles Times*.
barna.com

Founded in 2012, Boulder-based **GLOO**, LLC makes it easy for churches and faith networks to connect to, engage with and inform people so they can move to the next right step. Gloo connects to multiple sources of digital outreach, carefully matching people to churches and programs for hope, help, prayer and engagement. This work is done in partnership with leading faith campaign partners, equipping ministries and church networks. The goal is that churches using Gloo will see new people connecting with them each week. Gloo partners directly with Barna on a number of key research and equipping initiatives, including the Barna Access platform.

In addition, Gloo's platform grants access to personal growth resources, tools and innovations, including growth plans and assessments from respected research partners and professional associations.
gloo.us

Six Questions About the Future of the Hybrid Church

Created with Stadia, this data-driven journal will give you an update on what's working (and what's not) in digital-hybrid ministry.

Growing Together

Created with The Navigators, this three-part report reveals how God can use discipleship to nurture a resilient faith in you and the people you love. It also explores what day-to-day discipleship can look like.

Making Resilient Disciples Course

One of several video courses in our store, this training will show you how to prepare young Christians for the challenges they'll face as they seek to follow God in a digital world.

Tech-Wise Courses

Led by Andy Crouch, this online course helps leaders strength-en relationships in their own homes and equip the families in their congregations to design lives where technology plays a supporting role instead of a consuming role.